REAL ESTATE INVESTING

VOCABULARY OF TERMS

THE LANGUAGE OF THE DEAL

MEANINGS AND EXPLANATIONS

MICHAEL LANTRIP

Attorney | Accountant | Investor

MICHAEL LANTRIP

THE AUTHOR

Michael Lantrip, Attorney at Law, is licensed to practice law in Texas, North Carolina, Virginia, and the District of Columbia.

He has a B.B.A. in Finance from the University of Houston School of Business, and he has a Juris Doctor (J.D.) in Law from the University of Texas School of Law.

He is admitted to practice law in all Courts in Texas, North Carolina, Virginia, and the District of Columbia, as well as the U.S. Tax Court, U.S. Federal District Court, Eastern District of Texas, and the D.C. Court of Appeals.

He is a member of the National Society of Accountants.

He practices in the fields of Real Estate Law, Tax Law, Corporate and Business Law, and Wills, Trusts and Estates.

Formerly a Tax Examiner for the IRS, and a Tax Accountant for a Big 8 Accounting Firm, he has also been a Military Intelligence Analyst, News Director, Newspaper Reporter, Radio Announcer, Television Reporter, Anchorman, and Executive News Producer.

In addition to 37 years of practicing law, he built one of the first computerized Abstract Plants in Texas, using optical discs for storage, and operated his own Title Insurance Company, becoming an Approved Title Attorney for seven national Title Insurance Underwriters.

VOCABULARY OF TERMS

He has handled over 2,000 real estate closings.

As a Real Estate Investor, his activities have ranged from travel trailers to office buildings, and from on-campus condos to hundreds of acres of land.

Prior to his law career, he was a Radio Announcer at WQTE in Detroit during the "Motown" era, and he was a DJ at KIKK in Houston when it was named "Country Music Station of the Year" by Billboard Magazine.

He has written and produced more than 1,000 half-hour Television Newscasts.

He has written over 700 stories as a Newspaper Reporter.

He has logged over 8,000 hours on the radio.

He was named a Top Writer by Quora.com, where his Answers have been viewed over 500,000 times.

He is a Lifetime Member of Mensa.

He has written and published five other books:

1.) "How To Do A Section 1031 Like Kind Exchange"

2.) "50 Real Estate Investing Calculations"

3.) "Tax Cuts And Jobs Act For Real Estate Investors"

4.) "Your Best Business Entity For Real Estate Investing"

5.) "10 Other Real Estate Investments You Could Do"

All are available in print and digital on Amazon.

His Amazon Author Page is:

MICHAEL LANTRIP

www.amazon.com/Michael-Lantrip/e/B01N2ZRGUY

His Quora page is:

www.quora.com/profile/Michael-Lantrip-1

His personal website is MichaelLantrip.com.

VOCABULARY OF TERMS

INTRODUCTION

Real Estate Investing has its own language.

It's "the language of the deal."

We learn how to speak a language by listening to others speak it.

And that's where the problem comes in.

A very large portion of the words and terms being used for communication in the world of Real Estate are either incorrect, incomplete, or misleading.

And many words and terms are unknown to most investors.

And yet, you will be judged on what you say.

You will be judged harshly if it is not accurate.

And you will be judged favorably if it is clear, precise, and shows an understanding of the subject matter.

Ask yourself: "Do you know what you are talking about?"

The answer is primarily a matter of perception on the part of the listener, and secondarily a matter of your knowledge and understanding.

Make sure that you "know what you are talking about," and that people understand what you say.

The words that you use can be a red flag.

This problem is not your fault. You have wandered into this world, expecting it to have a "body of knowledge" and a rational and reasonable foundation, but it does not.

Certain ideas and concepts have become ingrained in the thinking and the language of Real Estate Investing through continued use, even though they are incorrect.

And they can cause you to be involved in situations where you say things that make you look foolish.

Make sure that you have the facts.

- "Pre-Approved" actually means that you have not been approved. In fact, it means that the person or committee that will make that decision has not even seen your application.

- Internal Rate of Return (IRR) is almost impossible to estimate accurately until after you have sold the investment. So it sounds impressive, but is totally impractical.

- There is no such thing as "clear title" to real estate. Know what you get instead.

- Signing a Deed In Lieu of Foreclosure back to the Lender might solve one problem, but will create another, maybe two, of having taxable income. Beware.

- A "Quitclaim Deed" is not a deed, and it does not transfer title to real estate.

- The idea that you can "abandon" property, and if you do, title reverts to someone else and the property becomes their responsibility, is totally ridiculous.

VOCABULARY OF TERMS

- Just having landlocked property does not grant you an "Easement of Necessity" to cross someone else's property.

- Obtaining title to property "by adverse possession" is so unlikely that it virtually never happens.

- There is no legal requirement that your company hold "an annual meeting."

- Family members **can** engage in an "arms-length transaction," it is **not** prohibited.

- There is no "Certificate of Title" to real estate.

- There really is a 0% Capital Gains Tax Rate.

- There is a "Dragnet Clause" in your Mortgage or Deed of Trust that can put a lien on your property for later-acquired debt and even unsecured debt.

- There are three types of Personal Guaranty, one is terrible, two are good.

The world of Real Estate Investing is filled with incorrect or incomplete information.

And when you discuss these subjects, you are sending a clear signal of your level of knowledge and understanding.

Many people have described to me deals that they were exploring, deals that they walked away from, because the other party "just didn't seem to know what he was talking about. Or if he did, he couldn't express it."

Or a situation where, "I couldn't explain it to him. He couldn't understand it."

MICHAEL LANTRIP

Real Estate Investing is not a closed community. It is open to everyone. And it does not pit one group against another. We are all in it together.

But we have to be credible and knowledgeable, and being able to speak the language is the first requirement.

Let this book be your Guide.

Read the definitions. Study the examples. Change the way you speak. Sound like a professional while you are working to becoming one.

If you have a question or comment, please contact me.

Michael@MichaelLantrip.com

Good Luck.

VOCABULARY OF TERMS

COPYRIGHT PAGE

Copyright 2020 Michael Lantrip.

All Rights Reserved.

Visit the author's website at www.MichaelLantrip.com

Visit Amazon's Michael Lantrip Author Page at:

https://www.amazon.com/Michael-Lantrip/e/B01N2ZRGUY

Publisher: ANDERSON LOGAN, LLC

First Edition

Version 1.0

ISBN 978-1-945627-12-5

This publication is designed to provide general information regarding the subject matter covered. Because each individual's legal, tax, and financial situation is different, specific advice should be tailored to those particular circumstances. For this reason, the reader is advised to consult with his or her own attorney, accountant, and/or other advisor regarding the reader's specific situation.

The Author has taken reasonable precautions in the preparation of this book and believes that the information presented in the book is accurate as of the date it was written. However, neither the Author nor the Publisher

MICHAEL LANTRIP

assume any responsibility for any errors or omissions. The Author and the Publisher specifically disclaim any liability resulting from the use or application of the information contained in this book, and the information is not intended to serve as legal, tax, or other financial advice related to individual situations.

VOCABULARY OF TERMS

DISCLAIMER

Although I am a lawyer, I am not your lawyer. I would be honored if I were, but I am not.

Reading this book does not create an attorney-client relationship between us. This book should not be used as a substitute for the advice of a competent attorney admitted or authorized to practice law in your jurisdiction.

CONTENTS

THE AUTHOR	ii
INTRODUCTION	v
ABANDONMENT	1
ABNORMAL SALE	2
Example	2
Another Example	3
ABSTRACT OF JUDGMENT	4
ABSTRACT OF TITLE	6
ACRS	8
ACCELERATION CLAUSE	10
ACCESS	12
ADJUSTABLE RATE MORTGAGE	13
Example	14
ADVERSE POSSESSION	14
AG USE EXEMPTION	17
Example	18
ANNUAL MEETING	18
APPRAISAL	19

VOCABULARY OF TERMS

APPRECIATION	21
Example	22
ARM'S-LENGTH TRANSACTION	25
AS IS	26
ASSESSED VALUE	27
ASSIGNMENT OF RENTS	28
ASSUMABLE LOAN	29
BANKER'S YEAR	31
BASIS	32
BUY-SELL AGREEMENT	35
CAP RATE	36
Example	36
CAPITAL GAINS	38
Example	40
CAPITAL GAINS TAX RATE	41
Example	42
CASH-ON-CASH RETURN	43
CERTIFICATE OF TITLE	49
CHAIN OF TITLE	50
CLEAR TITLE	51
CLOSING COSTS	51

CONSTRUCTIVE EVICTION	54
COST SEGREGATION	55
COUNTER OFFER	57
DAILY ACCRUAL AMOUNT	59
DEED	60
DEED IN LIEU OF FORECLOSURE	63
DEED RESTRICTIONS	64
DELINQUENT RENT	65
DEPRECIATION RECAPTURE	66
Example	67
DISCOUNTED CASH FLOW	68
Example	69
DRAGNET CLAUSE	76
DUE-ON-SALE CLAUSE	76
EARNEST MONEY	78
EASEMENT	79
ENCROACHMENT	80
EQUITY	81
Example	82
ESCROW	85
EVICTION	86

VOCABULARY OF TERMS

FAIR MARKET VALUE (FMV)	86
FEDERAL TAX LIEN	90
FIRST LIEN	91
FUTURE VALUE	92
Example	93
HOLDOVER CLAUSE	95
INDEPENDENT CONTRACTOR	96
INSTALLMENT SALE	97
Example	99
Another Example	100
INTERIM FINANCING	101
INTERNAL RATE OF RETURN	102
IRREVOCABLE TRUST	104
LATE FEES	105
LEASE-TO-OWN	107
LIVING TRUST	108
LOAN MODIFICATION	108
MASS APPRAISAL	109
MAGI	110
PRESENT VALUE	111
Example	112

OWNER FINANCING	116
PASS-THROUGH ENTITY	116
PERSONAL GUARANTY	118
POINTS	120
POWER OF ATTORNEY	120
PRE-APPROVED	122
PUBLIC NOTICE	123
QUITCLAIM DEED	124
REVOCABLE TRUST	124
RIGHT OF SURVIVORSHIP	126
SELLER FINANCING	127
STEPPED-UP BASIS	128
SUBORDINATE FINANCING	133
SUBSTITUTION OF COLLATERAL	134
TITLE INSURANCE	135
TITLE OPINION	136
VALUE	137
VOID	142
WRAPAROUND FINANCING	143

VOCABULARY OF TERMS

ABANDONMENT

In the world of Real Estate, "abandonment" is being defined as the act of just walking away from a property and declaring that you are giving up all ownership and other rights, and the ownership reverts to either the prior owner, or someone else, or to the State.

Don't get caught using this reference.

It's a fantasy. It doesn't happen.

If the property is in your name, you own it, and you have all of the legal responsibilities of ownership, and you will continue to own it and be responsible for it until you transfer the ownership to another individual or entity in the manner required by law, or until the property is sold at public auction, either to satisfy a judgment, or in compliance with a Court Order.

You cannot create a legal outcome, or accomplish anything, by just "walking away" from a property.

In fact, the law does not distinguish between you being present on the property or not present on the property, so even the idea of "abandonment" has no legal substance.

You either own the property, or you don't.

And if you do own it, you need to take care of it because you are responsible for it, and you cannot abandon it.

There is no legal process attendant to "disclaiming ownership" in real estate law.

ABNORMAL SALE

"Abnormal sale" is a term that is often misunderstood.

Knowing what an abnormal sale is can help you avoid using the term incorrectly yourself, and can help you push back if a Lender or Taxing Authority employee tries to use it against you.

First, let's look at a "normal" sale of real estate.

A normal sale of real estate is one that happens in the open market when willing sellers and buyers agree on a price. This price is referred to as the Fair Market Value (FMV), and the transaction is referred to as an arm's-length transaction. Consideration is exchanged and documents transferring title are recorded.

An "abnormal sale" is often described as one in which the price is very much higher or very much lower than other similar properties in the same neighborhood. And, **because of this price discrepancy,** the sale is eliminated from use as a "comparable sale" or from use to determine the overall average.

This is wrong!

EXAMPLE

There is a house in a neighborhood where the average price of houses is $225,000.

VOCABULARY OF TERMS

But this house sells for $130,000 because it is ugly, or is a log house, or is on a steep incline, or has a concrete yard.

This house sale will be declared an "abnormal sale" by an Appraiser, or by the Property Tax Appraisal clerk, or by the Bank, or whoever, and they will refuse to include it with all of the other sales, or acknowledge its value as related to the other house values.

But this sale is still a "normal" sale.

It took place in an open market where willing sellers and willing buyers determined the Fair Market Value (FMV).

The fact that some entities don't accept the price because they believe it should be something else, or because it doesn't fit their template, does not make it an "abnormal sale."

ANOTHER EXAMPLE

I can't leave this without giving an example of what an "abnormal sale" actually is, and why it meets the definition.

A homeowner gets behind in his mortgage payments, or he fails to pay his property taxes, or for some other reason he has violated the terms of his Mortgage or Deed of Trust, and the Lender posts the property for foreclosure, in a non-judicial foreclosure state.

The homeowner also cannot afford to pay his utilities and they are turned off, making the property uninhabitable, and the homeowner moves out.

The property sells at a foreclosure sale for $130,000 and it is in a neighborhood of mostly $225,000 houses.

This is an "abnormal sale" for two reasons.

The house was not sold on the open market, it was sold at auction.

The seller was not "willing," and was not even involved, and the buyers were not the entire group of people looking to buy a house. The buyers were a limited group of people who go to foreclosure sales. The others didn't even know that they could buy the house.

This sale meets the definition of an abnormal sale because it was a distress sale and it was not open to all of the available buyers.

ABSTRACT OF JUDGMENT

There is no such thing as "filing a lien," even though you hear that term often.

What is being filed is an Abstract of Judgment, and the multiple steps involved are very specific.

The "judgment" that we are dealing with is a Court Order signed by the Judge after the trial of a lawsuit. It may or may not be titled "judgment."

The Court Order states that the Plaintiff won the lawsuit, and describes what was awarded in terms of "damages." The judgment is then summarized in a separate document, by a process called "abstracting" the judgment, meaning the creation of an abstract, or summary, of the judgment decree.

VOCABULARY OF TERMS

This new document, called an Abstract of Judgment, is then filed in the Real Property Records of the county where the Defendant owns real estate.

Unless the real estate is the Defendant's personal residence, homestead, or is otherwise exempt from judgment, or levy and foreclosure, the Abstract of Judgment filing will automatically create a lien on the property.

This lien attaches to the property, and is referred to as a Judgment Lien.

Depending on the laws of the State where the Abstract of Judgment is filed, the lien created might be the type of lien that can be foreclosed on.

From this point forward, the process that is followed will depend on State law.

But, to summarize, in order to have an Abstract of Judgment, you must first have a Judgment.

In order to have a Judgment, you must first have a trial, or both parties must agree to enter an Agreed Judgment in order to settle the case.

In order to have a trial or Agreed Judgment, you must have a lawsuit filed.

So, it all begins with a lawsuit, and ends, if the Plaintiff wins, with an Abstract of Judgment.

But there is no such process as "Filing a lien."

Understanding this process and being able to reference it will make you much more credible when discussing real estate.

ABSTRACT OF TITLE

"Abstract" and "title" are two entirely different things, so it is unusual to have the two terms used together.

An Abstract of Title is a chronological listing of all of the "documents of record" that have a bearing on the ownership, or title, of a piece of real property.

The Abstract might include, as an Attachment, copies of the actual documents, but the Abstract itself is just the list of the documents.

The Abstract of Title is not a Certificate of Title, it is not an Opinion of Title, and it is not a Title. It is only an authoritative list of every document affecting title to the property from all of the relevant public documents available. It does not include documents that **have not** been "filed of record."

The documents that it does include will be found in many different places.

The most obvious source will be the Real Property Records of the county in which the real estate is located. These will be documents such as the Deed, Deed of Trust, Mortgage, Release of Lien, and any document with the property's legal description on it.

But there are other public records where documents are recorded that might affect the ownership of real estate without being specifically about the real estate, such as the Probate Records, where an owner has died, and the property was inherited. Often, the Attorney conducting the Probate will have the Clerk create a

VOCABULARY OF TERMS

Certified Copy of the relevant documents from the Probate, and file those Certified Copies in the Real Property Records. But this does not always happen, so those records must be searched.

There might also be lawsuits that resulted in a Judgment being entered against the owner of the property, and those records are kept in the lawsuit file in the relevant Court. In some States, the Judgment does not create a lien on the person's property when the lawsuit is decided unless the Judgment is also abstracted and filed as an Abstract of Judgment in the Real Property Records. In other States, the Judgment automatically creates a lien on all of the Defendant's non-exempt assets, whether or not the judgment is abstracted and filed.

So, there are many sources for the records that are searched in order to produce the Abstract of Title.

The Abstract is usually produced either by the office of an Attorney, or by a Title Insurance Company.

The person doing the work is called an Abstractor. It is a very specialized profession and the people doing it are highly qualified.

The Abstract of Title is also sometimes called a Certificate of Abstract.

But remember, it is not an Opinion of Title, or a conclusion concerning title, or an actual Title.

It is intended to be used for studying the condition of title and drawing a conclusion.

ACCELERATED COST RECOVERY SYSTEM (ACRS)

ACRS is all about Depreciation.

And if you understand Depreciation, you will know more than 90% of your fellow Real Estate Investors, and your knowledge will be apparent when you talk about it.

And the best part is that it is not complicated.

The Accelerated Cost Recovery System (ACRS) actually no longer exists.

It was created in 1981 and was replaced in 1986, but is still referenced.

What we have now is the Modified Accelerated Cost Recovery System (MACRS).

It is similar to the ACRS.

The MACRS is a method of depreciation that taxpayers are allowed to use in order to claim a larger amount of annual depreciation allowance in the early years of ownership of business property than they would be allowed to claim if they were using the Straight-Line Method, which is an equal amount each year.

For real property, the MACRS is not used for the main asset itself.

An apartment building is depreciated for 27.5 years, an equal amount each year, until the entire Basis in the property, usually the purchase price, has been claimed by the taxpayer as a deduction from income. This is Straight-Line Depreciation.

VOCABULARY OF TERMS

For a commercial building, such as a warehouse, this time period is 39 years.

But there are individual elements of the business asset that can be depreciated using MACRS.

This applies to the parking lot and all of the outside lighting, the furniture and fixtures, and any other item of property considered to be Section 1245 Property, as opposed to the classification of the main structure of the building as Section 1250 Property.

These items are also sometimes referred to as "personal property," but that does not mean that they are your personal items. The IRS divides all assets for depreciation purposes into two categories, real property and everything else, which it calls personal property.

The IRS also assigns a depreciable life to this personal property, and that life is either 5, 7, or 15 years.

In addition to being able to depreciate these assets over a shorter time period, and therefore recover the initial purchase price quicker, these assets can also be depreciated in an "accelerated" manner, hence the term "Modified Accelerated Cost Recovery System."

There are four methods of accelerated cost recovery (depreciation).

1.) Double Declining Balance (or 200% Declining Balance),

2.) 150% Declining Balance,

3.) Sum of the years digits, and

4.) Units of production.

So, to summarize, the system in use today is the Modified Accelerated Cost Recovery System, and there are four types, with straight-line not being one of them.

Some "experts" claim that the system was adopted because an asset deteriorates more rapidly in its early years. This is nonsense. Just the opposite is true. The asset remains like-new during its early years, and deteriorates rapidly during its latter years.

The real reason that the system was created was as an incentive for taxpayers to purchase new machinery and equipment, rewarding them with larger depreciation allowance in the early years to reduce taxes and help offset the cost.

Understanding and being able to discuss ACRS will make you a more credible investor.

Most Loan Officers don't know the information that you just read.

ACCELERATION CLAUSE

All real estate investors are operating under an acceleration clause, and few understand the circumstances that can trigger it, or what the consequences are.

When you finance a real estate transaction, if it is not a cash transaction, the transaction will create a situation where the loan amount is paid out over a period of time, with each payment being part interest and part principal, and with the debt being secured by the real estate.

VOCABULARY OF TERMS

The transaction will involve drafting and signing certain documents.

These documents might be a Real Estate Note or Promissory Note, a Mortgage or a Deed of Trust, or a Contract.

These documents will contain clauses, and the clauses will explain the terms of the transaction, and the obligations and rights of the two parties.

One or more of the documents will contain clauses in which the occurrence of certain events will trigger the right of the Lender to declare that the entire remaining principal balance of the obligation is immediately due and payable, and can result in Foreclosure of the property if not paid.

This is the "acceleration clause."

It accelerates the future payments of the obligation to the present time.

This clause protects the interests of the Lender, and that protection might be necessitated by a number of reasons.

1.) The Borrower has transferred title to someone else, but has not paid off the debt on the property.

2.) The Borrower has not paid the property taxes and has allowed a delinquency to exist, which is accruing interest and penalties, and will lead to a Tax Suit.

3.) The Borrower has allowed the property insurance coverage to lapse, and the lender has been required to purchase insurance coverage, for which the Borrower has refused to reimburse the lender.

4.) There has been damage to the property, which has not been repaired, impairing the value of the collateral that is securing the loan.

5.) The Borrower has ceased making regular payments, and after being given the legal notices to cure the default, has failed to do so.

The Borrower is not without rights and protections in the process. Both State and Federal statutes outline the procedure that must be followed by the Lender in declaring the entire principal balance immediately due and payable, as well as the steps required to foreclose on the property.

The concept of an "acceleration clause" is closely tied to the "due-on-sale clause," discussed later.

Most investors who are looking at property to buy never consider the possibility that the acceleration clause on the existing financing has already been triggered, and that they might be wasting their time.

ACCESS

Access is not just the ability to get to your property, it is the legal right that you own which enables you to do so.

If you own a piece of real estate, you must also have a legal right to move from the property to a public street or road, and back again.

This is called "legal access," also just called "access."

VOCABULARY OF TERMS

If the property abuts a public street or road, then you have access. There is nothing in between your property and the public street or road to impede your passage.

If the property does not abut a public street or road, then you must own an additional strip of real estate that connects your property to the public street or road, or you must own the right to travel over and across a strip of real estate that is owned by someone else, to enter and exit your property.

Normally, this would mean that you have an Easement over this strip of property.

There are many different types, or levels, of Easements, and you should read about them.

ADJUSTABLE RATE MORTGAGE

Also called an Adjustable Rate Loan, the Adjustable Rate Mortgage (ARM) is a financing arrangement that you have with a Lender in which the interest rate, and therefore the monthly or periodic payment, will adjust at certain intervals, based on some fluctuating standard amount, plus a constant stated adjustment amount.

The Index normally used is the Treasury Bill rate, or the Prime Lending Rate.

New loans are normally at a fixed rate for a number of years, usually five, and then the interest rate will adjust up or down, and then adjust again at certain time intervals, either one, two, or three years.

EXAMPLE

You bought a home for $330,000 and make a down payment of $30,000.

You obtained financing on the remaining $300,000 at a rate of 5% for a term of 30 years.

The interest rate is fixed for five years, and then is adjusted every three years to a rate that is 1.4% above the LIBOR Index for that date.

LIBOR is London Interbank Offered Rate.

Your initial monthly payment is $1,610.46.

On the fifth anniversary of the loan, the LIBOR rate is 5.8%.

Your lender adds 1.4% to this, sets your new interest rate at 7.2%, and runs a new Amortization Schedule that shows your monthly payment will now be $1,944.98.

Your interest rate has increased 2.2%.

Many loan agreements will have limits set on the amount of allowable increase at any one change date, usually 1% or 2%.

If your loan documents had such a limit, then the lower interest rate would apply.

ADVERSE POSSESSION

A popular misconception of Real Estate Law is that one of the ways people obtain title to property is by Adverse Possession.

VOCABULARY OF TERMS

This almost never happens.

While operating a Title Insurance Company, I did title searches on properties over a 16 year period, multiple times each day, each search involving looking at 20-30 documents in the chain of title.

I never saw a piece of Real Estate where anyone in the chain of title obtained that title under the law of Adverse Possession. Not one.

Adverse Possession is a means of acquiring title to real estate by establishing "actual, open, notorious, exclusive, hostile, and continuous" occupancy of the real estate for a certain period of time.

It sounds possible if you say it real fast, but it almost never happens, and looking at each individual element will show why.

- "Actual" means that you must actually be in possession of the property, either living there or using the property on a regular basis.

- "Open and notorious" means that you are possessing the property in a manner that is clear for everyone to see, and that your possession of the property demonstrates to an observer that you believe that you are the owner because you are acting like the owner of property would act.

- "Exclusive" means that you have not permitted anyone else to enter the property, and that you have attempted to prevent them from doing so, such as by fencing the property and putting up a locked gate, which also contributes to the "notorious" requirement.

- "Hostile" means that you have fought any claims by any other person to the property.

- "Continuous" means uninterrupted. And some of the State statutes require possession periods up to 40 years.

But the primary stumbling block to claiming title to property by adverse possession is that you must be making your claim based on some legitimate claim of "right of title," such as a signed document. So you can't just go to the Courthouse and look in the records and pick a bunch of properties and claim them. Or drive by a vacant lot, and decide to start paying taxes on it, and then say that it is yours.

The actual process of acquiring Title by Adverse Possession involves filing a lawsuit and asking the Court for a Declaratory Judgment establishing your ownership of the property.

During the more than 37 years of practicing law, I have never seen it.

The environment varies among States, but in the ones where I am licensed and attend the required number of Continuing Legal Education (CLE) courses each year, the State Bars are not even providing courses on the subject.

But your State might be different, so you should look into it.

VOCABULARY OF TERMS

AG USE EXEMPTION

"Agricultural Use Exemption," referred to as "ag use exemption," is a method whereby a property owner qualifies to have real estate that he owns appraised for property tax purposes on the basis of the use of the property for agricultural purposes.

This exemption is often combined with the same concept for property being used to grow timber, and the exemption is referred to as the "Ag/Timber Exemption."

The purpose of the property owner applying for and obtaining Ag/Timber Exemption is to lower the amount of property taxes assessed on the property.

Instead of the property being taxed on its Fair Market Value, it is taxed on the value of the timber, or the value of the hay that it will produce.

It can usually reduce a $5,000 property tax bill to about $500.

And it is available to investors who are just holding raw land for investment, not just for farmers or timber companies.

But the Exemption is granted to the owner of the property, based on the owner's use of the property, and a new owner must apply for a new exemption. So, if you are negotiating to buy a large tract of land, you might put a contingency in the Contract that depends on you being granted the Ag/Timber Exemption.

EXAMPLE

You own 100 acres of real property that you bought for $300,000 and you believe that it is "in the path of future development" outside a city on a major highway.

You want to hold it for a number of years as an investment and you want to reduce your holding costs as low as possible.

If you do nothing to change the category of the property and it is assessed for tax purposes based on its fair market value as potential commercial or residential development, your annual tax bill will be about $5,000 in an area with average property tax rates.

But if the property is part wooded and part open land, you can apply for an Ag/Timber Exemption, and have the property assessed based on the value of the timber growing on it and the value of the hay that can be produced by the open fields.

This will result in a much lower property valuation.

Your annual property taxes with the Ag/Timber Exemption will likely be in the range of two or three hundred dollars.

ANNUAL MEETING

Annual meeting refers to the meeting that takes place once a year for legal entities, such as LLCs, Partnerships, S Corps, and C Corps.

This is a meeting of the individuals holding an ownership interest in the entity.

VOCABULARY OF TERMS

Most people believe that annual meetings are an absolute requirement under law, and that the entity can lose its legal standing or status by failing to hold these meetings at least once a year.

But most State laws, if they have a requirement at all, only require that certain actions be taken "annually," such as the re-election of officers, but also include language such as "unless otherwise provided by the company's bylaws or operating agreement."

And, of course, the business statutes of most States allow for "any action that can otherwise be taken, can be taken by unanimous written consent of the parties involved."

So, what most business entities do, if they have a competent Attorney advising them, is just draft a "Resolution By Unanimous Written Consent" each year that includes all of the new actions that need to be authorized, and "ratifying" all of the actions that have previously been taken, have the document signed by all of the parties, and enter it into the file, or Minute Book, if one is being kept.

APPRAISAL

An appraisal is an attempt to determine the value of real property.

It is an estimate, not a determination of value.

And, of course, "it depends," and therefore the appraisal is actually an opinion.

And, as an opinion, there can be a number of different appraisals, and all of them can be correct.

The result will be determined by what you are needing to know.

1.) The amount of insurance coverage that is appropriate.

2.) The amount of damages to claim in the case of a loss.

3.) The amount on which Inheritance Taxes should be based.

4.) The amount for which the asset should be bought or sold.

5.) The amount to be asserted as the correct amount in a property tax protest.

6.) The separate value of each component, such as the land, the buildings, the standing timber, the commercial gravel pit, or whatever.

7.) The amount of compensation due to a property owner when the government takes the property for a highway.

8.) The amount on which to base the loan on the property.

The outcome will also be determined by which appraisal technique is used. There are three.

1.) Cost Approach. This is what it would actually cost to build the property.

2.) Income Approach. This is the capitalization of the annual income produced by the property.

VOCABULARY OF TERMS

3.) Sales Comparison Approach. This is based on an average of similar properties recently sold in the area.

And remember that an appraisal is very different from a property tax assessment.

See Assessed Value below.

APPRECIATION

"Appreciation" is the term applied to the increase in value of your real estate investment property.

Of course, if you've owned the investment property for a period of time, you can determine the increase in value by subtracting the Original Value from the Present Value.

To determine the **percentage** of Appreciation, you divide the Appreciation by the Original Value.

A = (PV − OV) ÷ OV, WHERE

A IS THE APPRECIATION PERCENTAGE,

PV IS THE PRESENT VALUE, AND

OV IS THE ORIGINAL VALUE

But you can't look at Appreciation in a vacuum.

It is also closely related to Future Value, and to Equity.

EXAMPLE

For Example, you bought a Fourplex for $400,000 a year ago and now you have determined by using the market Capitalization Rate, for this type of property, that it now has a value of $426,800.

A = (PV − OV) ÷ OV

A = (426,800 − 400,000) ÷ 400,000

A = 26,800 ÷ 400,000

A = .067

The investment property has appreciated in value 6.7% in one year.

FUTURE VALUE

But we are usually interested in determining the Appreciation that will occur in investment property that we are considering purchasing.

For this, we use the Future Value Calculation.

FV = PV x (1+ I), **WHERE**

FV IS THE FUTURE VALUE,

PV IS THE PRESENT VALUE,

1 IS 1, AND

I IS THE PERCENTAGE INCREASE FACTOR.

For Example, we buy a $400,000 Fourplex and

VOCABULARY OF TERMS

expect it to increase in value 6.7% each year.

$FV = PV \times (1 + I)$

$FV = 400,000 \times (1 + .067)$

$FV = 400,000 \times 1.067$

$FV = 426,800$

At the end of Year 1, your Fourplex will have appreciated in value to $426,800.

Now, for the Calculation on the second and subsequent years' appreciation, you use a new PV figure for the ending of the prior year, which is the same as the beginning of the current year.

In this Example for the second year we would use a PV of $426,800 because that is what it was at the end of the first year.

$FV = PV \times (1 + I)$

$FV = 426,800 \times 1.067$

$FV = 455,396$

At the end of your second year of ownership, your Fourplex will have appreciated to a value of $455,396.

Alternatively, you could multiply 1.067 times 1.067 and get 1.1385, and multiply 1.1385 times 400,000 and get the same number, 455,396.

Here is an online Calculator that you can use for Future Value calculations.

https://www.calculatorsoup.com/calculators/financial/future-value-calculator-basic.php

EQUITY

The above Calculation will serve you well if you pay cash for the investment property, but few of us do. We usually have debt on the property.

If you have debt on the property, then what you actually have that is appreciating in value is more important than just the Fair Market Value (FMV) of the property.

What you have that is actually appreciating in value is your Equity in the property.

This is the difference in the FMV of the property and what you owe on the property.

There is a Calculation for Equity.

E = FMV − MPO − L − OD, WHERE

E IS YOUR EQUITY IN THE PROPERTY,

FMV IS THE FAIR MARKET VALUE OF THE PROPERTY,

MPO IS THE MORTGAGE PAYOFF AMOUNT,

L IS LIENS ON THE PROPERTY, AND

OD IS OTHER DEBTS ON THE PROPERTY

A month after you purchase the property, the FMV will already have gone up, because that is what property does, and the MPO will go down, because each of your mortgage payments will be a combination of interest and reduction of principal. The reduction of principal amount

VOCABULARY OF TERMS

will reduce your MPO. The reduction will be small at the beginning, and huge at the end.

If you want to Calculate your probable Equity in the future, you would use the Future Value Calculation to determine the new amount of the FMV, and then use your Amortization Schedule that you received from your lender to get your Mortgage Payoff amount for the specific date you are calculating for.

Then plug the two numbers into the above Equity Calculation to determine your Equity at any point.

ARM'S-LENGTH TRANSACTION

A transaction that is "arm's-length" is one in which each party is looking out for his own best interest and there is no collusion involved in the ultimate outcome.

There is a mistaken belief that a transaction between the following parties would not be an arm's-length transaction.

1.) a husband and wife,

2.) a father and son, or

3.) a corporation and one of its subsidiaries.

This is incorrect.

If the outcome of the transaction is identical to one engaged in by two complete strangers, with the same result, then it is an arm's-length transaction.

The transaction does not require that the participants be unrelated and totally disinterested.

An arm's-length transaction only requires that the outcome is not influenced by personal considerations between the parties, but is what would be done by two willing participants in an open market, and the parties are dealing from equal bargaining positions.

It might be more difficult, but it is not impossible, and it is not prohibited.

AS IS

The term "as is" is used by the Seller of an asset to disclaim any and all warranty and representations regarding the item being sold.

The Buyer inspects the item, and if he buys it, he assumes all risks from that point forward.

The concept usually applies to personal property, but not to real property, if the real property is vacant land.

With real property, the transfer of ownership is evidenced by a written document, usually a deed, and that document is usually called a Warranty Deed.

The "Warranty" in the title means that the Seller is warranting (guaranteeing) that he owns the real property.

But he is not guaranteeing that a sinkhole will not develop the next day.

If there is a structure on the property, the structure on the property can be sold "as is" provided this provision

VOCABULARY OF TERMS

is stated in the written document that evidences the transaction.

"As is" has no single, universally accepted, legal definition. So if you are involved in such a transaction, add more information to the document describing exactly what you mean by the term.

Regarding the buying and selling of a personal residence, some States have laws that prohibit disclaiming any warranty regarding the structure. There is an implied warranty of habitability.

"As is" is not a defense against actual fraud, where the Seller intentionally misleads the Buyer, or knows that the Buyer has a misconception of significant importance and fails to correct the misinformation.

ASSESSED VALUE

This is the number that the Taxing Authority assigns to property in order to then calculate the amount of property taxes that must be paid by the owner. It applies to both real property and personal property.

It is not an appraisal of the Fair Market Value (FMV) of the property, nor is it intended to be. It is a number used for the purposes of tax assessment.

The FMV of the property might be used in determining the Assessed Value of the property, but that FMV number will usually not be based on an appraisal, but on a comparison with other real estate that is similar.

Each State has a different set of laws concerning how real property is assessed for tax purposes.

A popular method is for the Tax Appraisal District to declare that the FMV of your property is $600,000 and then calculate the Assessed Value at 80% of the FMV, and come up with a value of $480,000 on which taxes will be assessed. Then the local tax rate is applied to the $480,000 of Assessed Value.

A taxpayer will often miss an opportunity to lower his property taxes because he receives a tax bill that says his Assessed Value is $480,000 and he knows that his property is worth at least $500,000. He doesn't read the part that explains that assessments are based on 80% of value.

So he accepts the situation and pays the taxes, not realizing that the amount that he is really being taxed on is $100,000 too much.

Always look at the "assessment ratio", and calculate the actual number that they have assigned as the FMV of your property, not just the Assessed Value.

ASSIGNMENT OF RENTS

When a real estate investor gets a loan on a rental property, he will sign a number of legal documents, whether the transaction is a purchase or a refinance.

Depending on where you live, these documents will be called different things, such as Real Estate Lien Note, Promissory Note, Mortgage, Deed of Trust, or something else.

VOCABULARY OF TERMS

The lien documents will be filed "of record" in the Real Property Records of the County in which the property is located.

The investor will also sign another document called an "Assignment of Rents" which will probably not be filed of record along with the other documents, but kept in the Lender's files to be used if required.

With this document, the investor assigns his right to receive the rents from the property to the Lender. The purpose is to protect the Lender in case the investor stops making payments on the obligation, by authorizing the Lender to collect the rent and apply it to the Note.

When the Note goes into default, the Lender files the Assignment of Rents in the Real Property Records, obtains certified copies, and sends the certified copy by certified mail to the tenant, and instructs the tenant to begin making monthly payments to the Lender instead of the Owner.

ASSUMABLE LOAN

An assumable loan is one that can be assumed by another person without any material changes in the terms of the loan.

Most FHA and VA loans are usually assumable by their terms, but not all.

The fact that a loan does not have a "due-on-sale" clause in it does not mean that it is assumable.

And while a loan being "assumable" is a possibility, it is not a guarantee.

The decision is entirely up to the Lender, who will make sure that the assuming party can qualify for the loan, just like a new borrower would have to qualify for a new loan.

In many cases, if the interest rate has risen since the loan originated, the Lender will not approve the assumption, but will offer to initiate a new loan on the property in the amount of the remaining principal balance, or even more.

And in cases where the interest rate has fallen, a borrower would not be interested in assuming a loan with a higher interest rate anyway, unless he cannot qualify for a new loan, in which case he probably would not qualify with the Lender to assume the existing loan.

When loan assumptions occur, it is usually during a period of stable interest rates, and involving a borrower who can qualify for a new loan but who wants to save the expenses of generating a new loan, in addition to the time and hassle, and just pay the reasonable assumption fee of a few hundred dollars.

In all cases, the original borrower remains liable on the loan until the entire principal balance is paid off. This can be a problem because it will be carried on his credit report for that entire time, which could be upwards of 30 years.

VOCABULARY OF TERMS

BANKER'S YEAR

There are 365 days in the year.

Yes, I realize that you already know that.

But did you know that it takes the Earth 365 1/4 days to complete its orbit around the sun, not 365.

So, every four years we have to add one day to our year, making 366 days, in order to synchronize the calendar year with the solar year.

We stick that extra day at the end of February, giving it 29 days, and we call the year "Leap Year."

Of course, the rest of our months have either 30 or 31 days.

Remember the children's rhyme.

"30 days has September, April, June, and November;

All the rest have 31, except February, which has 28;

Except in Leap Year, when it has 29"

This has always (before computers) caused real problems for the Banking Industry.

So Bankers ignore all of this for their own personal interests, as they ignore many other truths.

A Banker's year has 12 months of 30 days each, for a total of 360 days.

You might see this reflected in your financing documents.

The problem is, in the real world, how many days are we dealing with if a document says "half a year?"

Well, it depends on where we are at the time in that year, and whether it is Leap Year.

But not in the Banker's Year.

It's 180 days no matter where you are in the year, or which year you are in.

So, to be fair to the Banker, it just works better this way in the world of finance, when all of the months are the same, and all of the years are 360 days.

Even if we have to pretend that's the way it is.

BASIS

If you own real estate, you have a "Basis" in that property.

There are three ways that your Basis in property comes into existence.

1.) You bought the property.

2.) You received the property as a gift, or

3.) You inherited the property.

PURCHASED PROPERTY

If you bought the property, your Basis is what you paid for the property.

VOCABULARY OF TERMS

If you've made any capital improvements to the property, this amount is added to your Basis, unless you identify the improvements separately and depreciate them on your Depreciation Schedule.

If you purchased a Duplex for $265,000 today, your Basis in that property is what you paid for it, plus any costs of acquisition, usually just your closing costs.

If you incurred $5,000 in acquisition costs, then your Basis in the property is $270,000.

If you spend $30,000 improving the property, then your Basis in the property becomes $300,000.

If you sell at this point, your Capital Gains will be the differences between your $300,000 Basis and your Net Sales Proceeds.

If you rent out the property, you will be allowed to claim an annual depreciation allowance, and deduct that amount from your rental income, and this Depreciation will lower your Basis in the property.

But let's assume that you assign a value of $25,000 to the land on which the Duplex is sitting, and subtract that out because land is not subject to depreciation.

That leaves a Depreciable Basis in the property of $275,000 which can be depreciated over a period of 27.5 years, resulting in an annual depreciation allowance of $10,000.

After you have rented the Duplex for five years and claimed $50,000 in depreciation allowance, your Basis in the property is $250,000 because you must deduct Depreciation from your Basis.

So, for property that you purchased, your Basis is the purchase price, plus cost of improvements, and minus depreciation allowed.

There is a very good Calculation for Basis, from my book "50 Real Estate Investing Calculations" that is available in ebook and paperback on Amazon.

$B = PP + CI - D$, WHERE:

B IS THE BASIS IN THE PROPERTY,

PP IS THE PURCHASE PRICE,

CI IS THE COST OF IMPROVEMENTS, AND

D IS THE DEPRECIATION ALLOWED.

For our Example above:

B = 270,000 + 30,000 − 50,000

B = 250,000

GIFTED PROPERTY

If you received property as a gift, your Basis in the property will be the same as the Basis of the individual who gifted the property to you.

INHERITED PROPERTY

If you inherited property, you might or might not receive a Step-up in Basis.

VOCABULARY OF TERMS

BUY-SELL AGREEMENT

A Buy-Sell Agreement is a written contract between or among owners of interest in a legal entity, usually Shareholders or Partners, that upon the occurrence of a certain event, ownership of an interest will transfer in a specified manner.

These Agreements are normally used when you set up an LLC with another person, and each of you own a 50% interest. If the other person dies, you probably do not want to then be in business with whoever inherits that other interest. So you have a Buy-Sell Agreement that says that you have the right to purchase the other interest at a specified price and under specified terms.

A Buy-Sell Agreement is also used to cover one of the owners filing for Bankruptcy protection, or just wanting to leave the business.

The Agreement might say that you will purchase the interest for the amount of the Capital Account of the other party. Or you might agree to pay ten times the average annual Net Income for the prior five years. And instead of paying cash, you might be permitted to sign a Promissory Note for the amount, payable over a certain period of time at a certain interest rate.

Other than the Cardinal Rule of never owning real property in your own name, this might be the most important thing you can do to avoid a disaster in your real estate investing career.

A Buy-Sell Agreement should be signed by all of the parties involved in the business ownership who might have an interest in the outcome of such an event.

In States with "community property" law, make sure that you have the spouse also sign the Agreement, because it will contain terms that contradict the community property laws.

CAP RATE

The Capitalization Rate (CR), referred to as the Cap Rate, is the ratio of the Net Operating Income (NOI) to the Fair Market Value (FMV) of the property.

The CR is your overall rate of return on the value of the asset.

There is a Calculation for Cap Rate.

CR = NOI ÷ FMV, WHERE

CR IS THE CAP RATE,

NOI IS THE NET OPERATING INCOME, AND

FMV IS THE FAIR MARKET VALUE OF THE PROPERTY.

EXAMPLE

For Example, if you have a $500,000 multi-family property that has a Net Operating Income of $65,000 the Calculation is:

CR = NOI ÷ FMV

CR = 65,000 ÷ 500,000

VOCABULARY OF TERMS

CR = 0.13

The Cap Rate for this property is 13%.

Investors in a particular market, of for a particular type of real estate investment, don't actually declare what their Cap Rate is, but they establish the Cap Rate by their decisions on how much to pay for an investment property that has a specific Net Operating Income.

In the above Example, investors in that market are willing to pay $500,000 for an investment property that has Net Operating Income of $65,000. That consensus among them creates the 13% factor as the market Cap Rate for property of that specific type in that specific price range in that specific market.

The Law of Supply And Demand will create the consensus.

So, you will hear references that say the Cap Rate is such-and-such for this type of property in this market.

One of the values of using the Cap Rate to compare different properties is that the NOI does not include debt service, an expense which will be different for every potential buyer, and using the Cap Rate allows for across-the-board comparisons of just the properties, with the same assumptions applied to each one.

In addition to using the Cap Rate alone to compare potential investment properties, you can use it in association with Cash Flow analysis.

A calculation based on Cap Rate and Discounted Cash Flow might give you even more valuable information.

CALCULATOR

You can quickly Calculate your Cap Rate with the following Free Calculator.

https://www.ajdesigner.com/php_capitalization_rate/capitalization_rate.php

1.) For "net operating income (NOI)" enter 65000 (no comma).

2.) For "value or cost (V)" enter 500000.

3.) Click "Calculate."

Your Cap Rate is 13%.

This is the same number that we got previously.

CAPITAL GAINS

Capital Gains is essentially the profit that you make when you sell real estate.

It also applies to personal property, but we will only deal with real estate here.

It is calculated as the difference between the Net Sales Proceeds, and the Basis in the asset sold.

The Net Sales Proceeds is calculated as the Sales Proceeds minus all of the expenses that were necessary to complete the sale.

The Basis is calculated as:

1.) purchase price of the property,

VOCABULARY OF TERMS

2.) plus capital improvements,

3.) minus allowable depreciation.

The Capital Gains tax rate is either 0%, 15%, or 20%.

(Yes, there is a 0% Capital Gains tax rate.)

Which tax rate of the three applies to you will depend on the amount of your other income for the same tax year in which the Capital Gains transaction happened.

But the three tax rates only apply to the portion of your Capital Gains that is referred to as the "pure Capital Gains."

Pure Capital Gains is calculated as:

1.) Net Sales Proceeds,

2.) minus the original Purchase Price, plus Capital Improvements.

The remaining portion of your Capital Gains was caused by the reduction in the Basis of the property that was caused by claiming the allowable depreciation on the property as an expense deduction against income, because claiming depreciation lowers the original Basis in the property and capital improvements.

And lowering the Basis increases the Capital Gains resulting from the calculation.

So, how do you account for this other portion of the Capital Gains resulting from the depreciation?

Well, you are required to isolate this amount, identify it as Depreciation Recapture, and pay a tax of 25% on it.

EXAMPLE

You bought a rental property for $320,000.

You assigned a value of $45,000 to the land (which is not depreciable) and depreciated the remaining $275,000 for 27.5 years as Residential Rental Property, claiming $10,000 per year in depreciation.

After seven years the property has more than doubled in value and you sold it $740,000 and incurred $20,000 in transaction costs, leaving Net Sales Proceeds of $720,000.

Your Basis in the property at the time of sale is $250,000. This is $320,000 minus $70,000 claimed depreciation.

Your Total Capital Gains is $470,000. This is $720,000 minus $250,000.

I would have to know your tax profile to determine whether you are into the 20% Capital Gains tax bracket, and whether or not some of the Capital Gains falls into the 0% Capital Gains tax bracket, so we will just assume that you are in the 15% bracket.

But before you pay the tax on the Total Capital Gains, you pay the Depreciation Recapture tax on the amount of depreciation that you claimed.

That $70,000 times 25% is $17,500. This is your Depreciation Recapture tax.

The remaining $400,000 is taxed at the Capital Gains rate of 15%. This amount is $60,000.

VOCABULARY OF TERMS

Your total tax liability is $77,500 on $470,000 of Capital Gains and Depreciation Recapture.

This is an effective rate of about 16.5%.

CAPITAL GAINS TAX RATE

The Capital Gains Tax Rate for Short-term Capital Gains is tied to the Taxpayer's individual income tax bracket.

But the Long-term Capital Gains Tax Rate is either 0%, 15%, or 20%, and depends on the Filing Status of the Taxpayer, as well as the Taxpayer's total taxable income.

SINGLE (S):

0% = $0 to $39,375

15% = $39,376 to $434,550

20% = $434,551 and up.

MARRIED, FILING JOINTLY (MFJ):

0% = $0 to $78,750

15% = $78,751 to $488,850

20% = $488,851 and up.

These tax rates are marginal tax rates, and not flat tax rates, so your Capital Gains might be taxed at two different rates.

In addition, higher-income Taxpayers may also have to pay an additional 3.8% Net Investment Income Tax (NIIT).

EXAMPLE

Your "total taxable income" on which your Capital Gains Tax Rate is based includes the Capital Gains income itself.

So, for instance, if all of your income from sources other than your Capital Gains is $30,000 and you sell an asset with a Long-term Capital gains is $100,000, then your total taxable income would be $130,000.

This would put you in the 15% Capital Gains Tax Rate category.

But that does not mean that the entire $100,000 would be taxed at 15%.

If you are Single, the $30,000 of taxable income other than your Capital Gains would be taxed at the ordinary income tax rate of 10% for the first $9,525 and 12% for the next $20,474.

The total tax on the $30,000 is $3,409.38.

When the $100,000 is added and taxed at the appropriate Capital Gains Tax Rate, the first $9,375 in taxed at 0% because the 0% Capital Gains Tax Rate goes from $0 total taxable income to $39,375 total taxable income.

But starting at $39,376 total taxable income, and going through $130,000 total taxable income, the Capital Gains Tax Rate is 15%.

VOCABULARY OF TERMS

The amount of total taxable income is $90,625 and the tax amount is $13,593.75.

So, although you had $100,000 in Capital Gains, $9,375 of it was actually taxed at 0%.

The numbers are different for Married, Filing Jointly (MFJ).

CASH-ON-CASH RETURN

Many investors believe that ROI is less important than the return that you receive on the cash that you invest, because cash is what you have of your own to put into the investment.

The Cash On Cash Return (COCR) is the relationship between a property's Cash Flow (CF) and the Initial Capital Investment (ICI).

Cash Out versus Cash In.

And we have a Calculation for that.

COCR = CF ÷ ICI, WHERE

COCR IS THE CASH ON CASH RETURN,

CF IS THE PROPERTY'S CASH FLOW, AND

ICI IS THE INITIAL CAPITAL INVESTMENT REQUIRED TO ACQUIRE THE PROPERTY.

First, let's establish that ICI is the initial cash down payment and all of the costs of acquiring the property, usually the closing costs that are detailed on your HUD-1 Settlement Statement, for which you paid.

Now, we need to determine how we will define Cash Flow (CF) because CF seems to have a different definition, depending on the purpose for which it is being used.

Cash Flow is actually the cash left over after you take the monthly cash income from the property, and pay all of the monthly expenses of the property.

In other words, it is cash in, less cash out.

It even has its own Calculation.

CF = I − E, WHERE

CF IS CASH FLOW,

I IS ALL OF THE CASH INCOME, AND

E IS ALL OF THE CASH EXPENSES.

The Cash Flow Calculation is used to create a profile of a property so that you can compare two properties.

Therefore, Cash Flow should only include those characteristics of a property that all other properties also have. Otherwise, you cannot compare them.

So, the Income of the property should be the cash produced by the operation of the property.

Some Cash Flow Calculations include as "Income," proceeds from a loan obtained and secured by the property.

VOCABULARY OF TERMS

And some Cash Flow Calculations include as "Income," interest on funds held by the owner of the property that came from the past operation of the property.

These two items should not be included in Income. They do not measure the character or the operation of the property.

Also, some Cash Flow Calculations include Debt Service (DS) as one of the Expenses that are deducted from the Cash Income.

How does this make sense? DS is a measure of the credit worthiness of the person who obtained the loan, if it is a measure of anything. You can't use it to compare two properties with two different owners. The interest portion of the payment on the DS will be deductible as an expense, but the remainder of the payment represents payment on the principal, which is not an operating expense.

And finally, some Cash Flow Calculations fail to include a number for Cap Ex.

No, it is not a monthly cash expense (at least you hope it is not), but it is a real expense that will occur at random intervals and will reflect the true long-term Cash Flow of the property.

And including a Cap Ex figure in your Cash Flow Calculation will allow you to compare rundown properties with properties in good condition, because the rundown properties will require more capital expenditures than the properties in good condition.

Your most accurate Cash Flow Calculation, and your most accurate Cash On Cash Return Calculation, will include an allocation for Cap Ex.

Of course, you can leave out the Cap Ex Expense if you want, but if you are negotiating with a Lender, they will want to see it in there, because they've had the experience of having a customer come in and tell them that they can't make the note payment because they have to put on a new $15,000 roof.

It means the Lender will have to either take the property, or make a second loan to cover the roof.

So, let's go back to Cash On Cash Return (COCR).

Let's say you can buy a Fourplex for $400,000 and you can get a 75% loan, meaning that your cash down payment will be $100,000. Your closing costs will be $10,000 and you anticipate spending another $15,000 to increase the income capability of the property to its highest possible level.

Your total cash investment will be $125,000.

You Calculate your Cash Flow to be $23,040.

You haven't yet accounted for Debt Service, but you can Calculate your COCR at this point.

$COCR = CF \div ICI$

$COCR = 23{,}040 \div 125{,}000$

$COCR = 18.43\%$

But your most accurate COCR is what you have left to put in your pocket to return what you took out of your pocket.

VOCABULARY OF TERMS

Your Debt Service is $1,500 per month, $18,000 per year.

This leaves you a true Cash Flow of $5,040.

COCR = CF ÷ ICI

COCR = 5,043 ÷ 125,000

COCR = 4.03%

Your Cash On Cash Return is a good tool for comparing two properties, but probably not as good when you are making a decision to buy and hold a property for ten years.

The COCR Calculation does not take into account the annual increase in Cash Flow as you raise the rents, or the time value of money, both of which will change your Calculation.

The Calculator that I have chosen to use is the Payback Period Calculator, because it will allow you to track these two items.

CALCULATOR

Now that you understand the concept of Cash on Cash Return, let's do a Calculation.

https://www.ajdesigner.com/php_cash_on_cash/cash_on_rate.php

1.) For "annual cash flow (ACF)" enter 23040 (no comma).

2.) For "cash invested (CI)" enter 125000.

3.) Click "Calculate."

Your COCR is 18.43%, which is what we got doing it by hand.

You can change the Calculation to solve for different unknowns.

There is another Calculator that will combine your Cash on Cash Return information with your Payback Period, and I think you will find it interesting and useful because the two are closely aligned.

http://www.calculator.net/payback-period-calculator.html

1.) For "Initial Investment" enter 125,000.

2.) For "Cash Flow" enter 23,040.

3.) For "Increase" enter 5%.

4.) For "Number of years" enter 10.

5.) For "Discount Rate" enter 7.3%.

6.) Click "Calculate."

As you can see, your Payback Period is 4.886 years.

Your Discounted Payback Period is 6.176 years.

And your annual return for the Cash Flow is 17.39%.

Pick one of your own investments and put the numbers in to see what you get.

VOCABULARY OF TERMS

CERTIFICATE OF TITLE

A Certificate of Title is a document issued by a governing entity, or a document that is authorized to be issued by a third party, certifying ownership of property.

But it only applies to personal property, such as a vehicle.

There is no such thing as a Certificate of Title to real estate.

The confusion occurs because of two other documents called "Abstract of Title" and "Title Opinion."

See those definitions.

You will see incorrect information in Dictionaries saying that a Certificate of Title is issued by a title company.

This is completely incorrect.

A "title company" is actually a Title Insurance Company. They issue an insurance policy on the title to the property that you are buying. But the type of insurance policy that they issue does not insure you against events that will happen in the future, like an automobile insurance policy. The Title Insurance Policy insures you against events that have already happened, in the past, that were not discovered in a search of the chain of title to the property, and that will cause you to suffer a loss.

This is why a Title Insurance Company searches title to real estate. It is to determine if the title is "insurable" for them at a low enough risk to issue a policy.

The fact that a Title Insurance Company searched title to the property and issued an Owner's Policy of Title Insurance does not mean that the property has clear title.

Almost no real property in America has clear title. But it does have title that a Title Insurance Company will accept the risk of insuring.

CHAIN OF TITLE

Chain of Title refers to the consecutive transfers of title from Original Land Grant to the present holder of title.

In the commercial environment today, we usually trace title back about 30 years.

Title Insurance Companies do this research before issuing a Policy of Title Insurance on the property.

You, as the insured party in that policy, will not receive any of the paperwork involved in the searches.

If you would like to have copies of all of the documents in the chain of title, what you want is an Abstract of Title With Documents Attached.

The Chain of Title produced by the Title Insurance Company is just for their files, to determine if they are willing to take the risk of insuring title, and to be used to defend claims against the title if one should come up in the future.

VOCABULARY OF TERMS

CLEAR TITLE

There really is no such thing as Clear Title.

In the United States, with the early Land Grants, the promoters, the crooked Politicians, the illiterate population, and even honest mistakes, every parcel of land has some cloud on the title from the past 240 years.

What we usually deal with is what is called "insurable title."

That means that the Title Insurance Company has searched the public records for all of the documents that affect the title to the property. And they have concluded that although they cannot show that title is clear, they believe that the items that might affect the ownership of the property held by the Seller are so unlikely to come up, that they are willing to pay the Buyer for any loss he may suffer as the result of such an event.

Title is not clear, but it is insurable.

It's the best we can do.

CLOSING COSTS

Closing costs are one of the most-discussed, and least-understood, aspects of the real estate investing process.

When a property changes hands, meaning that it is sold by one person or entity to another, the entire process is usually handled by a Title Insurance Company or a Real Estate Closing Attorney.

For this discussion, we will assume that it is done by a Title Insurance Company.

The individual doing the Closing is called the Closer, usually a State-licensed Escrow Officer.

The Closer will prepare a Closing Statement, sometimes also called a HUD-1.

This is where you will find the closing costs.

There might be a single Closing Statement with separate second and third pages for the Seller and the Buyer, usually called the Borrower, so as to account for the loan funds in the mix. Or there might be separate, but similar, Closing Statements for each. The law requires that each person's information remain confidential.

The Buyer and Seller can agree between themselves which one will be paying which of the closing costs. Sometimes, even the Lender can agree to pay some of the closing costs, but there are also government rules prohibiting this.

If the Sales Agreement does not provide otherwise, here are the typical closing costs allocated to each party.

SELLER.

1.) Premium for Owner's Policy of Title Insurance.

2.) Attorney fees for preparation of Warranty Deed, and any Releases of Lien required as part of the process of clearing title, as well as the recording fees for the documents.

3.) Real Estate Transfer Tax, if the State has one.

VOCABULARY OF TERMS

4.) Real Estate Sales Commission if a Realtor was involved.

5.) One-half of the Title Insurance Company's fee for closing the transaction.

6.) Pest Control Inspection, if one was required.

7.) Loan Payoff, if there was any debt on the property.

8.) Survey, if one was involved.

9.) Any fees charged by the Title Insurance Company to the Seller for services or considerations provided, such as accepting an existing Survey instead of requiring a new one.

10.) The amount of Property Taxes that are accrued and unpaid, which amount will be transferred to the Buyer so that the Buyer can pay the entire year's amount when due.

BUYER

1.) All costs charged by the Lender associated with acquiring the new loan on the property, including inspections and certifications.

2.) Attorney fees for preparation of the legal documents required by the Lender associated with the loan, as well as the recording fees.

3.) One-half of the Title Insurance Company's fee for closing the transaction.

4.) Premium for Lender's Title Insurance Policy.

5.) Fees charged by the Title Insurance Company for providing additional coverage not required by law, as well as any additional escrow services.

Real Estate Closings are usually a matter of State law, and will vary somewhat. The State has become heavily involved in the Title industry, and is fostering new laws that attempt to make the Title Insurance Company responsible for certifying personal matters over which they have no control, such as where the Buyer got the money for the down payment.

So far, these new social policies are not working out very well.

CONSTRUCTIVE EVICTION

Usually a Tenant will have a written Lease which will outline the conditions that will lead to the right of the Landlord to evict the tenant from the premises.

Sometimes the occupancy will be without a written document and will be what is considered a month-to-month tenancy.

And under both situations, the State government and the Federal government also have a myriad of laws that govern the situation, so many laws that there is an entire body of law called "Tenant-Landlord Law."

The main focus of everything is on "eviction."

Sometimes, the Landlord will want to evict the Tenant, and sometimes the Tenant will want to claim that an eviction has, in effect, occurred.

VOCABULARY OF TERMS

This latter situation is called constructive eviction.

The Tenant is still in the property, but some condition or situation has come about that makes it impossible for the Tenant to enjoy the premises in a manner that is considered his right under law.

The Tenant might claim that the Landlord has allowed the property to fall into such disrepair that it is uninhabitable in some other way.

Under such a situation, the Tenant will usually withhold rent payments until such conditions are remedied.

In some situations, the Landlord wants to get rid of the Tenant and does not have a legal reason to do so, and will actually create a situation which amounts to constructive eviction, like turning off the utilities, making the property uninhabitable.

Constructive eviction is not actual eviction. The Tenant is not removed from the premises, and is usually still occupying the property. But the Tenant claims that the property is no longer habitable, and the situation is the same as if he had been evicted.

COST SEGREGATION

Cost Segregation is the process of taking all of the costs of material and labor that went into creating a real estate asset, and segregating those items into classes of depreciation that are long (27.5 years and 39 years) and classes of depreciation that are short (5, 7, and 15 years).

For example, a $10M Apartment Complex is depreciated over a period of 27.5 years.

After allocating $1M to the cost of the land, the remaining $9M provides an annual Depreciation Allowance of about $325,000.

This is the amount of depreciation, not an out-of-pocket expense, that is deducted from the property's income before the taxable amount is determined.

So the depreciation actually shields about $325,000 of income from taxation.

But this amount can be increased by doing a Cost Segregation Study, which identifies those items other than the basic structure of the building that can be classified as 5-year, 7-year, and 15-year depreciable items.

These are items like all of the parking lot, outside lighting, interior doors, carpet, and many other non-structural items.

In most cases, a Cost Segregation Study will identify about 30% of the total cost of the property as available for shorter depreciation lives.

If just $3M of the $9M were depreciated for an average term of 10 years, this would provide $300,000 in annual Depreciation Allowance.

With the remaining $6M being depreciated for 27.5 years, and providing about $220,000 in annual Depreciation Allowance, the total amount of annual Depreciation Allowance after doing a Cost Segregation Study would be $520,000.

VOCABULARY OF TERMS

This is an increase of $195,000 each year.

The ability to claim Depreciation and shield income from taxation is one of the main reasons that people choose to invest in real estate.

But a Cost Segregation Study is not simple or cheap.

It requires a combination of two professionals, an accountant and an engineer.

It is a very detailed study, and will include such small minute items as the size and total lengths of Romex used in wiring the building.

This is not something that an accountant can determine on his own, and even if he could, the IRS would not accept his determination.

An Engineer could do it, but he could not apply the appropriate section of the Tax Code.

So a true Cost Segregation Study is one that is compiled by a group that includes accountants, preferably a CPA, and a group of engineers, preferably a Construction Engineer.

The cost of a Study like the one we are talking about will run $30,000 and up, but as you can see, it will quickly pay for itself.

COUNTER OFFER

When a real estate property is for sale, the Seller is offering to sell the property for a certain price and under certain conditions.

This is the offer of the Seller.

It is made to the general public.

If someone steps up and agrees to buy at that price and under those conditions, the Seller has a binding legal obligation to sell, conditioned on the Buyer satisfying the requirements.

But in most situations, the Seller will receive an offer to purchase, at a certain price, and under certain conditions, which are different from the price and the conditions of the Seller's offer.

The Seller is no longer obligated to sell to this particular potential Buyer under the terms of his original offer, but now had been presented with a counter offer.

The counter offer has the effect of saying, "No, I don't accept your offer, but here is my offer to you."

It is important to understand how "offer" and "counter offer" work, and how they affect each other and the parties involved.

If the Seller now rejects the counter offer, then there are no continuing obligations on the part of either party. They are in the negotiating stage, which might or might not lead to a deal.

A smarter method of negotiation would be to say, "I am not rejecting your offer, but would you be willing to do such and such?"

If the Seller refuses, you can still accept his original offering.

VOCABULARY OF TERMS

DAILY ACCRUAL AMOUNT

The Daily Accrual Amount that we are considering is the daily amount of interest that is being added to your mortgage each day since the last payment was made.

Most definitions and calculations presented to you to determine Daily Accrual Amount will not tell you what you need to know.

For instance, if you have a $300,000 loan at 6%, the common method suggested is to multiply 6% times $300,000 and get $18,000. Then divided $18,000 by either 365 days or 360 days (we'll use 360) and get $50.00.

But this is not correct, because the interest due and the principal reduction is different for each period.

To determine the Daily Accrual Amount on your mortgage, look at the current payment period that you are in. Then look at the interest portion of the payment that is due in that period. Divide that number by the number of days in the month, or simply by 30 if your Lender is using the Banker's Year method. The number that you get will be the amount of interest that is accruing each day for the payment period that you are in at that point.

The Daily Accrual Amount will be significant when you are selling a property, and you are paying off the mortgage on the property. Your lender will provide a Payoff Amount to the Closer.

It will be the Remaining Principal Balance after you made your last payment on the mortgage, plus an amount of interest that is accruing daily.

This way, the Closer can calculate the amount to be sent to the lender, no matter which day of the month the Closing takes place, without having to get a new Payoff Amount from the lender.

DEED

A deed is the document that the Seller of real estate signs and gives to the Buyer to evidence the transfer of ownership of the property.

The name of the document and the required content will be determined by the laws of the State in which the property is located.

But there are a number of universal requirements for all deeds.

The necessary elements of a deed are:

1.) Grantor: the individual or entity who owns the property and is transferring it.

2.) Grantee: the individual or entity to whom the property is being transferred.

3.) Property Description: sufficient to identify the property owned by the Grantor to the exclusion of all other property.

4.) Consideration: no longer required in some States, and not even required to be stated correctly in any States, and usually recited as "Ten dollars and other good and valuable consideration."

VOCABULARY OF TERMS

5.) Habendum clause: exact rights being transferred by the Grantor to the Grantee, such as "To have and to hold ..."

6.) Signature: also called "execution," usually required in front of Notary Public but, surprisingly, not always. Some States even allow you to stop a couple of Gomers passing by and have them sign as "Witnesses." Don't do it. Always notarize signatures, while complying with other State law requirements.

7.) Delivery: this completes the transaction. Recording in the public records is not required in some States for the deed to be valid and complete, but is required to give notice to the public of the transfer of ownership.

Rather than having one basic deed, there are many different types of deeds, depending on what is being accomplished.

A General Warranty Deed is one in which the Seller "warrants," or guarantees title to the property.

A Special Warranty Deed is one in which the Seller guarantees title to the property, but only guarantees that he has done nothing to mess up the title while he owned the property, and does not guarantee that something did not happen prior to him acquiring the property that will negatively affect the title.

A Deed Without Warranty does not warrant, or guarantee, title to the property. If you buy it, you take the risk. You can mitigate the risk by acquiring an Owner's Title Policy from a Title Insurance Company, which will first search the title to determine its condition.

A Deed Without Warranty is what should be used instead of a "Quitclaim Deed."

Yes, "Quitclaim" is one word, and there is no such thing as a "Quick Claim" anything.

In fact, a "Quitclaim Deed" is not even a deed.

Look at the elements of a deed listed above.

Now think about what a "Quitclaim Deed" says.

It says, in effect, "I don't even claim that I own an interest in this property, but if I do, I hereby transfer that interest to you."

A Quitclaim Deed is not a document of conveyance, it is a document of disclaimer of interest in favor of someone else.

The overriding requirement of a valid deed is the intent to convey title to the property. The Granting clause says, "I hereby grant and convey."

The Quitclaim Deed intent is to disclaim interest in a property.

But people continue to try to use the document, so some States have amended their Real Property Code to deal with the Quitclaim Deed problem, and while not acknowledging that it is a deed, they allow its acceptance as transferring interest if certain other factors are present, or not present, and they sometimes require the passage of time, with the minimum being one year and the average being four years.

As the owner and operator of a Title Insurance Company, I never insured nor closed on property with a Quitclaim Deed in the chain of title.

VOCABULARY OF TERMS

Why would I insure ownership transferred from someone who says in writing that he doesn't even claim to own the property?

And why would you accept a deed that says that?

DEED IN LIEU OF FORECLOSURE

When a Borrower has defaulted on the loan that is secured by his real property, the Lender has a legal right to foreclose on the property and take it back.

But if the Borrower accepts the reality that there is nothing he can do to prevent this, he is likely to deed the property directly to the Lender, using a deed called a Deed In Lieu Of Foreclosure.

It saves the Borrower from having a Foreclosure showing on his credit record, as well as causing additional costs for the Lender, for which the Borrower is responsible.

But it can cause bigger problems for the Borrower, even resulting in taxable income, and in some cases, two different taxable incomes.

First, understand that the IRS looks at the transaction of deeding the property back to the Lender as a sale, with the Sales Price being the Fair Market Value (FMV) of the property at the time of the transaction.

If the FMV of the property is $260,000 and the Borrower owed more than that to the lender, say $300,000, the difference is considered a type of income known as Cancellation of Debt (COD) income.

The $40,000 would be considered ordinary income, and would be taxed at the Borrower's marginal tax rate.

This is one type of possible income.

If the Borrower has owned the property for quite a few years, and has just been refinancing it periodically, he might even have a low Basis in the property due to all of the depreciation taken.

If his Basis in the property is $200,000 at the time of the transfer, he would have a Capital Gain of $60,000 to report.

And the portion of this gain that was due to the depreciation claimed would be considered Depreciation Recapture, and would be taxed at 25%.

So, a Deed In Lieu Of Foreclosure can be more of a problem than a solution.

DEED RESTRICTIONS

A deed restriction allows you to sell real estate, and still control its future use.

Deed laws vary by State, but there will usually be a section where the Seller is allowed to place restrictions in the future on the use of the property he is selling.

VOCABULARY OF TERMS

For instance, if someone is selling a parcel of real estate next to where they live, and they want to make sure that there will never be a mobile home on the property, they can place a restriction in the deed that prohibits mobile homes ever being placed on the property.

If they want to make sure that someone doesn't start operating a garage on the property, or uses it to park tractor-trailers, they can also prohibit these activities.

Some deed restrictions might lower the FMV of the property by reducing the number of available uses, and therefore the demand for the property.

But in most cases, sensible deed restrictions will make a property more valuable, as well as holding or increasing the values of nearby properties.

DELINQUENT RENT

Delinquent rent is not necessarily rent that is not paid when due.

That rent payment is just late.

"Delinquent" is a legal term.

The Lease between the Landlord and Tenant will describe the point at which the unpaid rent becomes "delinquent."

There might be a provision that first describes the rent as "late," and assesses a "late fee" of a certain amount.

Then there will be a provision that describes at what point "late" rent becomes "delinquent" rent.

Delinquent rent will usually be the basis for an eviction procedure, so it is very important that the Lease be clear and specific about the terms and the time periods.

It is a good idea to have a Lease that was created by an Attorney in your State to provide for the exact manner in which you would like to deal with late and delinquent rent, as well as eviction.

The cost of a few hundred dollars for such a Lease is much less costly than the loss of six months of rent.

If you do not have a Lease, or have a month-to-month tenancy, everything will depend on the laws of your State.

DEPRECIATION RECAPTURE

Depreciation Recapture is a process whereby the IRS levies a tax on the amount of Depreciation that an owner of business real estate has claimed while using the real estate to produce income.

The Depreciation is an "allowance" that is claimed as an expense and deducted from the property's income before the taxable amount of income is determined.

It is not a cash expense, but is an "allowance" based on the price paid for the real estate.

Residential rental property is depreciated over 27.5 years.

VOCABULARY OF TERMS

Commercial real property is depreciated over 39 years.

Upon the sale of the property on which Depreciation is claimed, a Depreciation Recapture tax of 25% is assessed on the amount that has been claimed.

But it is not in addition to the Capital Gains tax. It is actually part of the Capital Gains that is calculated, and is taxed at the different rate.

EXAMPLE

You bought a rental property for $320,000.

You assigned a value of $45,000 to the land (which is not depreciable) and depreciated the remaining $275,000 for 27.5 years as Residential Rental Property, claiming $10,000 per year in depreciation.

After seven years the property has more than doubled in value and you sold it for $740,000 and incurred $20,000 in transaction costs, leaving Net Sales Proceeds of $720,000.

Your Basis in the property at the time of sale is $250,000. This is $320,000 minus $70,000 claimed depreciation.

Your Total Capital Gains is $470,000. This is $720,000 minus $250,000.

I would have to know your tax profile to determine whether you are into the 20% Capital Gains tax bracket, and whether or not some of the Capital Gains falls into the 0% Capital Gains tax bracket, so we will just assume that you are in the 15% bracket.

But before you pay the tax on the Total Capital Gains, you pay the Depreciation Recapture tax on the amount of depreciation that you claimed.

That $70,000 times 25% is $17,500. This is your Depreciation Recapture tax amount.

The remaining $400,000 is taxed at the Capital Gains rate of 15%. This amount is $60,000.

Your total tax liability is $77,500 on $470,000 of Capital Gains and Depreciation Recapture.

This is an effective rate of about 16.5%.

DISCOUNTED CASH FLOW

Discounted cash flow is, quite simply, the value in today's dollars of cash that will be received periodically into the future.

You absolutely cannot make decisions about real estate investing without understanding this concept. It makes it possible for you to compare all of your projected numbers, both income and expenses, as if they were today's dollars.

Let's look at the definition.

Discounted Cash Flow (DCF) is a Calculation of the Present Value (PV) of future streams of cash flow, based on an interest rate used as a discount factor.

It is similar to the concept of Present Value that determines the present value of assets with a known value in the future.

VOCABULARY OF TERMS

But the Discounted Cash Flow Calculation is for a stream of **periodic** payments.

It is really the inverse of the Compound Interest concept. Instead of starting with a present value, and adding in interest and interest-on-interest going into the future, we are taking a future amount, and pulling out an interest factor and an interest-on-interest factor from a future amount as we bring it back to the present.

EXAMPLE

Let's assume that you have projected a stream of payments that you expect to result from an investment property, such as Cash Flow.

You have a multi-family property that is creating monthly Cash Flow of $2,400 and you want to know the present value of two years of such payments.

You have placed a time value on the use of money in your set of circumstances at 12%. In other words, you are willing to pay 12% for the use of other people's money because you know you can make a profit using that money in your business activities. Therefore, the Time Value of Money for you is 12%.

The monthly Interest rate factor of 12% annual interest is 1%.

Let's discount the value of the first twelve months of Cash Flow.

For the first month, the value is $2,400 because you have the money in your hand now, assuming that you collect rents on the first day of the month.

To determine the present value of $2,400 received a month from now, you discount it by the 1% interest rate that you have assigned as your time value of money.

$PV = CF \div (1 + I)$, where

PV is the Present Value,

CF is the Cash Flow amount, and

I is the Interest rate factor you have assigned to the time period.

PV = 2,400 ÷ (1 + .01)

PV = 2,400 ÷ 1.01

PV = 2,376.24

So, the Discounted Cash Flow value of the $2,400 that you will receive at the beginning of next month is $2,376.24 today.

To discount the Cash Flow for the third month, the Calculation is slightly different.

$PV = CF \div (1 + I)^n$, where

PV is the Present Value,

CF is the Cash Flow amount,

I is the interest rate factor you have assigned, and

n is the number of periods you are discounting for.

VOCABULARY OF TERMS

The Calculation is the same as above, except that you are receiving the CF at the beginning of the third month and discounting it back for two months instead of one.

PV = 2,400 ÷ [(1 + .01) (1 + .01)]

PV = 2,400 ÷ (1.01 × 1.01)

PV = 2,400 ÷ 1.0201

PV = 2,352.71

So, your third month Cash Flow of $2,400 has a value today of $2,352.71.

You see the pattern here, so I'll run quickly through the rest.

Fourth: 2,400 ÷ 1.0303 = 2,329.42

Fifth: 2,400 ÷ 1.0406 = 2,306.36

Sixth: 2,400 ÷ 1.051 = 2,283.54

Seventh: 2,400 ÷ 1.0615 = 2,260.95

Eighth: 2,400 ÷ 1.0714 = 2,240.06

Ninth: 2,400 ÷ 1.0828567 = 2,216.36

Tenth: 2,400 ÷ 1.093685 = 2,194.42

Eleventh: 2,400 ÷ 1.104622 = 2,172.69

Twelfth: 2,400 ÷ 1.115668 = 2,151.18

The total amount of the twelve Discounted Cash Flows is $27,583.93.

The undiscounted amount would be 12 x 2,400 = $28,800.

The difference is $1,216.07, which is 4.22% less.

The difference between the stated amount and the discounted amount for the second year of payments would be even less.

If you just look at the 13th Cash Flow amount, you will see.

$PV = CF \div (1 + I)^n$

$PV = 2,400 \div [(1 + .01)(1 + .01)(1 + .01)(1 + .01)(1 + .01)(1 + .01)(1 + .01)(1 + .01)(1 + .01)(1 + .01)(1 + .01)(1 + .01)]$

$PV = 2,400 \div (1.01 \times 1.01 \times 1.01 \times 1.01 \times 1.01 \times 1.01 \times 1.01 \times 1.01 \times 1.01 \times 1.01 \times 1.01 \times 1.01)$

$PV = 2,400 \div 1.126825$

$PV = 2,129.77$

The Present Value of that $2,400 monthly Cash Flow a year from now is $2,129.77, a difference of $270.23.

Discounted Cash Flow becomes important when you are looking at your Cash on Cash Return (COCR) on your investment.

See the explanation of COCR.

$COCR = CF \div ICI$, WHERE

COCR IS YOUR CASH ON CASH RETURN,

CF IS YOUR CASH FLOW FOR THE PERIOD, AND

ICI IS YOUR INITIAL CASH INVESTMENT.

VOCABULARY OF TERMS

If your ICI was $160,000 for this multi-family property that is producing $28,800 in annual CF:

COCR = CF ÷ ICI

COCR = 28,800 ÷ 160,000

COCR = 18.0

So, your Cash on Cash Return for the first year would be 18.0%.

But since you put all of the $160,000 into the investment up front, and received the Cash Flow over a 12-month period, a more accurate calculation would be to use the Discounted Cash Flow method.

COCR = CF ÷ ICI

COCR = 27,583.93 ÷ 160,000

COCR = 17.24%

This is for the first year. The amount would be lower for the second, and the third, and so forth.

The Discounted Cash Flow method will also give you a more accurate estimate of your Payback Period.

PP = ICI ÷ CF

PP = 160,000 ÷ 2,400

PP = 66.67

The Payback Period is 66.67 months using the undiscounted Cash Flow method. That's five years, six months and 20 days.

To do the same Calculation for Discounted Cash Flow, we would need to know the amount for each month for the same period, add them together, and divide by the total number to get the average, and use that number.

Instead, we'll just use that 13th payment that we calculated above.

PP = ICI ÷ CF

PP = 160,000 ÷ 2,129.77

PP = 75.125

So, just using a single one-year-old Discounted Cash Flow, the Payback Period is pushed out to 6 years, 3 months and 4 days.

There are many reasons for using Discounted Cash Flow when comparing numbers in the present with numbers in the future. You will always get a more accurate Calculation.

CALCULATOR

Now that you understand how to use Discounted Cash Flow, here is a Free Calculator that will do it for you.

https://www.calculatorsoup.com/calculators/financial/present-value-cash-flows-calculator.php

1.) For "Interest Rate" enter 1 to indicate the monthly rate of 1% that reflects our 12% annual discount rate.

2.) For "Compounding" enter 1 to indicate that we only want the discount to be applied monthly.

VOCABULARY OF TERMS

3.) For "Cash Flow at" select "Beginning" to indicate when in the month the payment is received.

4.) For "Number of Line" select 10 just for this Example.

5.) For "Periods" enter 1.

6.) For "Cash Flow" enter 2,400.

7.) Click "Calculate."

You will get a chart showing the Discounted Cash Flow for each of the monthly amounts of $2,400 and a total for all.

Look at Period #10, which represents the tenth month of payments that we are discounting, and you will see that the Discounted Cash Flow is $2,194.42.

This is exactly the same amount that we got in the above Calculation that we did by hand.

So, we did OK.

However, this Calculator can do Calculations that, while I might be able to do them, I would never be able to explain them to you.

For instance, you can use this Calculator to discount future monthly payments that are not even, or that are even, but include something else occasionally such as a principal payment, or a late payment.

You just plug in whatever that amount will be in the appropriate "Period" line.

For this Calculator you only have to make sure that the payments are all at the same interval, and the same discount rate is applied throughout.

DRAGNET CLAUSE

A Dragnet Clause is a paragraph in a Deed of Trust or Mortgage in which you are pledging a specific piece of property as collateral for a loan.

The clause says that the collateral that you are pledging, usually real estate, will also secure any additional debt that you might owe to the Lender, including any future money that the Lender might loan you.

In some States, those future debts also include any debt that the Lender might acquire from someone else to whom you owe a debt. This has the effect of turning your unsecured debt with someone else, into secured debt with this Lender, secured by your real estate.

The Lender could just purchase your delinquent credit card debt for pennies on the dollar, because credit card companies almost never spend any money to litigate collections of these debts.

You could end up having your real estate foreclosed on for a debt that you originally created with someone else.

This is an onerous condition for a Lender to place on a borrower, and many Courts have refused to enforce such clauses if the dispute results in litigation.

DUE-ON-SALE CLAUSE

The due-on-sale clause is a statement in the Mortgage or Deed of Trust securing the financing on

VOCABULARY OF TERMS

your real estate that says if you sell the real estate, the debt on the real estate is immediately due and payable.

There is a popular misconception that there is a real question about whether the due-on-sale clause should be a concern for someone who sells mortgaged property, because the Lender doesn't really care as long as they are receiving payments.

But the financing document doesn't say anything about whether or not they care, if you commit an act that triggers the due-on-sale clause, the clause is triggered, the maturity of the Note is accelerated and matured, and the Principal is immediately due and payable.

It can't be undone, there is no act that reverses it.

The borrower is engaging in wishful thinking, and this is not the way a real business professional thinks.

The world of finance is conducted on strict business principles.

There are State and Federal laws that govern the conduct involved, and provide both civil penalties and criminal sentences for violations.

If you sell an encumbered asset without first paying off the debt, you could be doing what the law calls Hindering A Secured Creditor.

If your Mortgage requires you to notify the Lender and obtain permission before selling or encumbering the real estate and you do not, you could be committing Fraud.

EARNEST MONEY

Earnest Money is the cash deposit that is made by the potential Buyer of real estate when he signs the Sales Contract with the Owner of the property.

There is usually either a Realtor, Attorney, or Title Insurance Company involved, and sometimes all three. The deposit should be given to the Title Insurance Company or, in some cases, the Attorney. The Realtor should never be holding an Earnest Money deposit.

The purpose of Earnest Money is reportedly "evidence of a good faith intention on the part of the Buyer to complete the transaction."

However, the Sales Contract is usually written with contingencies so broad or vague that the potential Buyer can usually just say something like he could not get financing, or the property turned out to be unsuitable for his purposes, and take back his money and "walk away."

So Earnest Money has nothing to do with "good faith intention."

At one time, Earnest Money was essential to creating a valid Sales Contract because it provided the "consideration" necessary to form a binding Contract, but that is no longer the case. The "consideration" required is now stated to be the "mutual considerations" of the Buyer promising to buy, and the Seller promising to sell. This is kind of silly because without this, you wouldn't have a deal requiring consideration anyway.

In real estate transactions entered into by seasoned professionals, there will be Earnest Money involved, and the Seller will not accept the "walk away" contracts, so

VOCABULARY OF TERMS

that if the Buyer does not go through with the deal, he will definitely forfeit the Earnest Money. That's the purpose of having Earnest Money deposits today, to compensate the Seller if the Buyer is wasting everybody's time by not going through with the deal.

Earnest Money is usually placed into the hands of a third party. The Seller does not get it, and the Realtor does not get it.

It will go to either the Attorney handling the transaction, or the Title Insurance Company that will be insuring the property, and doing the Closing.

The party holding the Earnest Money is considered a "Fiduciary" under most State laws, and there are both State and Federal laws governing how the money is handled.

There will be a written agreement concerning what will happen to the money, when, and under what conditions.

EASEMENT

Easements are one of the major sources of misunderstanding about real estate.

An Easement is a legal right of one party to travel across the property of another party.

Usually an Easement is created in a legal document where the owner of the property grants the right.

Sometimes a Court will create an easement after a lawsuit is filed by the person requesting the Easement.

There are many different types of Easements and they are created in accordance with the laws of the State where the property is located, so for any additional specific information you should refer to the laws of your State.

But there is one thing that you can look out for.

Many dictionaries and legal articles are describing an "Easement of Necessity" as one in which you have the right to cross the property adjacent to yours if you do not already have access to a public road.

This is not correct.

No individual has the right to declare an Easement in favor of himself under any circumstances.

If you have property that is "landlocked" you have the right to go to Court and ask the Court to create an Easement because of your situation. And the Court will probably do it.

But you do not already have this right.

ENCROACHMENT

Encroachment is when a structure on your property crosses over your property line and onto the adjacent property, or a structure on the adjacent property crosses over the property line onto your property.

In the situation of encroachment onto your property, you do not have any rights in regard to the structure, except to file a lawsuit and compel the removal of the encroaching portion.

VOCABULARY OF TERMS

A situation often considered Encroachment, but which is not, is when the adjacent property owner builds a fence that is beyond his property line and is actually located on your property.

In this situation, you own the fence.

It was built on your property and became part of your property.

You can do what you want with it, although doing so will probably lead to a dispute that is more trouble than it is worth, but the law in your State is probably on your side.

EQUITY

Equity is the value you have in your real property investment.

There are two ways to look at it, as "investment equity" and "cash equity."

Investment equity is the difference between the FMV of the property and what you owe on the property.

Cash equity is what would have left on the table if you sold the property today for its Fair Market Value (FMV) and used the proceeds to pay off all of the debt on the property.

There is a Calculation for that, and it comes from "50 Real Estate Investing Calculations" which is available in digital and print from Amazon.

$E = FMV - MPO - L - OD$, WHERE

E IS YOUR EQUITY IN THE PROPERTY,

FMV IS THE FAIR MARKET VALUE OF THE PROPERTY,

MPO IS THE MORTGAGE PAYOFF AMOUNT,

L IS LIENS ON THE PROPERTY, AND

OD IS OTHER DEBTS ON THE PROPERTY.

EXAMPLE

If you bought a $210,000 Duplex, paying $50,000 down, $5,000 closing costs, and getting a $160,000 mortgage, then your Equity in the property is $55,000 (50,000 plus 5,000).

At the time of purchase, the FMV is presumed to be what you paid for the property, and you paid $210,000 to the Seller and $5,000 to the closing agent and others, for a total of $215,000.

$E = FMV - MPO - L - OD$

$E = 215,000 - 160,000 - 0 - 0$

$E = \$55,000$.

But even after you buy the property, you can Calculate your Equity at any time by using the above Calculation.

VOCABULARY OF TERMS

If you've held the property for at least a year, two of the four elements making up Equity have probably changed, and possibly all four.

Let's say you have held the property for three years.

By looking at comps, you determine that the FMV is now $255,000 because the property has appreciated in value about 6% each year, and because you have added a new furnace.

You have made 36 mortgage payments and the principal portion of these payments have reduced your payoff by $6,500.

You replaced the furnace at a cost of $6,000 and the company is allowing you to make payments on the bill in return for you granting them a lien on the property until it is paid, and the balance on the furnace bill is $4,500.

Your property taxes have accrued will be due and payable soon, and that amount will come to about $1,200.

So, the calculation now looks like this:

E = FMV − MPO − L − OD, WHERE:

E IS EQUITY,

FMV IS FAIR MARKET VALUE,

MPO IS MORTGAGE PAYOFF AMOUNT,

L IS LIENS, AND

OD IS OTHER DEBT.

$$E = 255{,}000 - (160{,}000 - 6{,}500) - 4{,}500 - 1{,}200$$

$$E = 255{,}000 - 153{,}500 - 4{,}500 - 1{,}200$$

$$E = \$95{,}800$$

Your Equity has gone up from $55,000 to $95,800 in three years, an increase of $40,800.

The increase is due to asset appreciation and mortgage paydown.

The $40,800 increase in Equity represents a 74.18% increase in three years, which is almost 25% per year. Of course, that does not take into account the time value of money.

And, of course, this Calculation is your Equity in the property if you plan to hold the property for more years into the future.

The amount of Equity that you would realize if you sold the property is a different number.

The $95,800 amount is not what you would receive in a check at the closing table if you sold the property.

You would have transaction costs to be deducted, such as Sales Commission, a Survey, a Title Insurance Policy for the Buyer, legal costs for document preparation, escrow fees, and others.

The total transaction costs could be as high as $18,000.

That would still leave you with Equity of $77,800, an increase of $22,800.

VOCABULARY OF TERMS

Your three-year increase percentage would be 41.45% instead of 74.18%, and your annual increase would be 13.8% instead of 25%.

Remember, in the truest sense, Equity is the actual value that you have in your real property, which is expressed in the number of dollars you could put in your pocket if you sold it.

ESCROW

In the world of real estate, Escrow is the process by which all of the parties involved in a transaction place signed documents and money in the hands of an independent third party, along with a signed Escrow Agreement, which details what is to be done, how it is to be done, and when it is to be done.

The Escrow Agent is also a Fiduciary and is bound by the laws thereof.

This is not the same as a Real Estate Closing by a Title Insurance Company or by a Real Estate Attorney.

The Escrow Agent does not perform a professional function or generate documentation that becomes part of the transaction.

An Escrow Agent just follows the instructions provided by the parties in the Escrow Agreement.

EVICTION

Eviction is the legal procedure by which a Tenant is forced to vacate the premises of the property that is being rented or leased.

The action will be premised on the conditions contained in the signed Lease or, if there is no Lease, on the laws of the State where the action takes place.

Sometimes the Landlord wants to get rid of the Tenant, but the Tenant has a right to remain as long as he pays the monthly rents and does not violate any of the terms of the Lease.

In this situation, the Landlord will make the premises uninhabitable in some way like turning off the utilities, or changing the locks on the doors.

This action is called "Constructive Eviction" and it is illegal.

FAIR MARKET VALUE

Fair Market Value (FMV) is a term used by Appraisers to describe the price at which a real property would change hands between a willing Buyer and a willing Seller in an open market where it was offered for a reasonable period of time.

The determination is often used to set the amount of compensation due a property owner when his property is condemned and taken by the government.

VOCABULARY OF TERMS

It is also used as a factor, along with a formula, when a government taxing authority assesses the amount or property taxes due on an asset, both personal property and real property.

But for real estate investors, it is a term used to declare what a property is worth.

The Fair Market Value (FMV) of a property is usually determined by the dynamic of supply and demand.

The definition of FMV as the price at which a willing Seller and a willing Buyer agree to transfer ownership of the property is correct.

But that is difficult to predict, and it isn't actually what the FMV of the property is for you, it's what the FMV is for two other people.

But this definition is one Fair Market Value, and you can determine it by looking at sales comparisons in your area for similar property.

But you want to Calculate the FMV for you.

The Calculation for determining what the FMV of the property is for you, if you know your Cap Rate, is:

FMV = NOI ÷ CR, WHERE

FMV IS THE FAIR MARKET VALUE OF THE PROPERTY,

NOI IS YOUR NET OPERATING INCOME, AND

CR IS YOUR CAPITALIZATION RATE.

If you have determined that the CR available to you with other comparable investments is 10%, and you are looking at a Duplex with an NOI of $30,000, and want to calculate the FMV:

FMV = NOI ÷ CR

FMV = 30,000 ÷ 0.10

FMV = 300,000

The FMV of this Duplex, based on your 10% Cap Rate, is $300,000.

However, you might not have a Cap Rate that you are comfortable using, but you know other numbers related to the property, such as the Gross Rent Multiplier (GRM).

The GRM is also a product of supply and demand.

If Fourplexes in your area with units that rent for $1,250 each are selling for $600,000 then you can calculate the GRM.

GRM = FMV ÷ GPI, WHERE

GRM IS THE GROSS RENT MULTIPLIER,

FMV IS THE FAIR MARKET VALUE, AND

GPI IS THE GROSS POTENTIAL INCOME.

GRM = 600,000 ÷ 60,000

GRM = 10

VOCABULARY OF TERMS

The investors in this area are paying ten times the GPI for multi-family properties.

With this knowledge, and the knowledge of how much the units are renting for, you can Calculate the FMV of a property.

FMV = GRM x GPI, where

FMV is the **Fair Market Value** of the **property**,

GRM is the **Gross Rent Multiplier**, and

GPI is the **Gross Potential Income**.

If you found a Fourplex with two units renting for $750 and two renting for $950, your GPI is (2 x 750) plus (2 x 950) times twelve.

1,500 + 1,900 = 3,400 x 12 = 40,800.

We plug that into the Calculation and use a GRM of ten.

FMV = GRM x GPI

FMV = 10 x 40,800

FMV = 408,000

Your Fourplex will have a Fair Market Value of $408,000 based on the Gross Rent Multiplier of ten that is the standard in that market for that type of property.

The Calculations for Fair Market Value are just guidelines for you to use to make your own decision about your next investment.

You might be faced with a totally different situation.

If there are only five seasonal-rental properties between the Interstate and a popular stretch of beach, and you own three of them, you will likely pay whatever you have to pay to get the other two. Paying over the Fair Market Value and raising rents 25% across the board because you control the market could be a good business decision.

The Real Estate Investing Calculations are just to help you make the decision that is right for your particular situation.

I refer you to another of my books, "50 Real Estate Investing Calculations," available in digital and print from Amazon.

FEDERAL TAX LIEN

A Federal Tax Lien is a lien placed on an individual's or an entity's personal property or real property by filing a Notice of Federal Tax Lien in the Public Records of the County of residence of the taxpayer, or County where the asset is located, or both.

The Lien is usually filed by the Internal Revenue Service (IRS), and is usually filed because the Taxpayer is delinquent in the payment of Federal Income Taxes, but can also result from the failure to pay Payroll Taxes or Estate Taxes.

The Federal Government may proceed to the Collection Process on the underlying liability, which could result in the foreclosure of the property, but they

VOCABULARY OF TERMS

usually just wait because their Lien is not one that can be wiped out, even by Bankruptcy, and it is also usually accruing penalties and interest, so they prefer to spend no money on collection, knowing that they will eventually be paid.

A Federal Tax Lien priority is placed after any existing tax liens for local property taxes and special assessments.

In the special case of a Lender foreclosing on a debt that was created to purchase the property, the Lender can avoid assuming the liability of the Federal Tax Lien by giving notice to the IRS for a certain amount of time and allowing the IRS to initiate foreclosure proceedings. After the time period has expired with no action by the IRS, the foreclosure can proceed and the Lender can take back the property without the Lien attached.

This does not wipe out the liability of the Taxpayer to the IRS.

FIRST LIEN

A First Lien is a lien that is first in priority in the event that all secured debts on the property are paid off.

A First Lien is usually the lien that is securing the debt that was created in order to purchase the property, as well as any refinancing of that debt.

If the property were sold at a Foreclosure Sale, the available Net Sales Proceeds would first be applied to pay off the First Lien.

Any remaining money would then be used to pay off any Secondary Liens, in order of their filing in the public records.

If any funds are remaining after the costs of the Foreclosure are paid, and the liens are paid off, the money will go to the Owner of the property.

The holder of a Second Lien that is in default can also foreclose on the property, but anyone purchasing the property would take it subject to the existing First Lien.

A First Lien is also sometimes called a First Mortgage.

FUTURE VALUE

Future value is, of course, the value of your real estate in the future.

One of the main reasons for investing in real estate is to increase your wealth through the yearly appreciation in property value.

The property will go up in value over the long term. It might go down in some years. It will increase in different amounts in different years. But over time, it will go up in value.

There are many estimates of the historic annual increase in value, but the one that I find has the most credibility is 6.7%.

You wouldn't be using this number in 2008, but it is probably good today.

VOCABULARY OF TERMS

The Calculation that you would use to determine Future Value is the same regardless of the number you use.

This Calculation is from my book, "50 Real Estate Investing Calculations," available in digital and print on Amazon.

***FV = PV x (1 + I)*, WHERE**

***FV* IS THE FUTURE VALUE,**

***PV* IS THE PRESENT VALUE, AND**

***I* IS THE PERCENTAGE INCREASE.**

EXAMPLE

Let's assume that you have a $400,000 property and you want to know what it will be worth each of the next five years, and at the end of that time, if it increases 6.7% each year.

FV = PV x (1 + I)

FV = 400,000 x (1 + .067)

FV = 400,000 x 1.067

FV = 426,800

The property will be worth $426,800 at the end of Year 1.

Then you take the new value that you just calculated, treat it as the new PV, and Calculate the value for Year 2.

426,800 x 1.067 = 455,396 at the end of Year 2.

And you continue to do that for each year.

455,396 x 1.067 = 485,908 at the end of Year 3.

485,908 x 1.067 = 518,464 at the end of Year 4.

518,908 x 1.067 = 553,201 at the end of year 5.

You can continue to create these Calculations for ten years, or even more, but at some point it becomes random, because the Calculations are initially based on an assumption, then the results are compounded with another assumption, and so forth, and the margin of error increases exponentially.

If you just want to know the potential value after five years, based on an annual increase of 6.7%, you can just multiply 6.7% to the fifth power and then multiply the answer by the original property value.

1.067 x 1.067 x 1.067 x 1.067 x 1.067 = 1.383

400,000 x 1.383 = 553,200

The property would be worth $553,200.

CALCULATOR

Now that you understand what the Future Value Calculation is, what it's used for, and how it works, here is a Free Calculator that you can use for quicker results.

https://www.calculatorsoup.com/calculators/financial/future-value-calculator-basic.php

1.) For "Number of Years" enter 5.0.

2.) For "Interest Rate" enter 6.70.

VOCABULARY OF TERMS

3.) For "Present Value" enter 400,000.

4.) Click "Calculate."

Your Future Value Calculation will be $558,655.39.

You will notice that in the above Calculation with the same information, our Future Value was $553,200.

This is not a mistake.

The difference is because the Calculator is compounding the 6.7% rate monthly, and we used annual compounding in the above Calculation.

This Calculator also allows you to do partial years; in other words, a number of months.

If you want to do the Calculation for three years and nine months, put in 3.75 for the "Number of Years" and get $523,893.34.

Play with the Calculator and see what else it can do for you.

HOLDOVER CLAUSE

This is a section of a Real Property Lease which describes what will happen when the term of the Lease expires, and it covers the possibility that the Tenant remains in the property.

Holdover may be strictly prohibited, and the clause will provide that the Landlord may evict the Tenant, or that the Landlord may move the Tenant's possessions out of the property and change the locks, provided this does not violate State or Federal law.

Most Leases will provide for the Tenant to continue to occupy the premises under certain circumstances, and conditioned on certain payments.

The Tenant will be in a month-to-month tenancy, and each advance payment will only ensure the following month's occupancy.

The Holdover Clause will describe the terms that will prevail if the Landlord does permit the Tenant to continue occupancy month-to-month, but the Tenant will rarely have any rights at all compared to the rights enjoyed under a 12-month Lease.

INDEPENDENT CONTRACTOR

An Independent Contractor is not a "contractor" in the sense of being a Builder.

The "contractor" designation just means that he is entering into a Contract with you to perform some function in return for payment.

The "independent contractor" status just means that he is not one of your Employees.

He is self-employed and contracts to do the work for you, but using his own methods and making his own decisions. He is not working under your direction as to when he will show up and as to methods used to perform the task. You only control the required results.

VOCABULARY OF TERMS

An Employee, on the other hand, is working under your direction.

The difference is critical because if you have an Employee, you are subject to State and Federal laws concerning almost everything about the relationship, but primarily concerning liability, the wages, tax withholding, Social Security payments and deposits, providing insurance, and paying for future unemployment compensation.

For Real Estate Salespersons, to become an Independent Contractor under Federal law, you must:

1.) have a written contract that states that you will not be treated as an Employee for tax purposes,

2.) have a real estate license, and

3.) be compensated on the basis of performance, and not on the hours worked.

However, you will still be subject to a significant amount of supervision because the Realtor is legally liable for your actions.

INSTALLMENT SALE

An Installment Sale is where the property is sold and instead of the Seller receiving all of the Sales Price, the money is paid in "installments," usually by the month.

There are two basic reasons that an Installment Sale comes about.

The first reason is a business reason and the second reason is a tax reason.

The business reason might be that the Seller does not want to receive all of the money at one time, but wants a situation where he will have future income for a specific period of time.

Or, the Buyer might not have the cash to pay for the property in full, or even the down payment, and/or might not have the credit required to obtain a loan on the property.

The tax reason is that the Seller might have a large amount of equity in the property and might not want to receive all of the Sales Price at one time and have to pay the large amount of Capital Gains taxes, and possibly Depreciation Recapture taxes at one time.

Whatever the situation, in an Installment Sale, the Buyer will make a down payment and sign a Promissory Note requiring monthly payments at a specific interest rate for a specified period of time.

The payments will be in the amount necessary to pay the interest due that month on the remaining principal balance, and to pay an amount reducing that same principal balance. So the payments will be made up of both interest and principal, and the ratio will change each month, while the total amount of the payment remains constant.

For the Seller, the tax liability will be calculated in the first year on the amount of the down payment received, plus the principal portion of each monthly payment received.

VOCABULARY OF TERMS

EXAMPLE

Let's assume that you bought a 40-acre tract of land ten years ago for $750 per acre, a total purchase price of $30,000.

This is your Basis in the property.

Now you sell the property for $100,000 on January 1, 2020.

You receive $20,000 down, and you agree to finance the balance of $80,000 for ten years at 6%, with monthly payments.

You will receive $888.16 Monthly payments.

The first year you will receive a total of $9,770.

The Interest income portion will be $4,264.

The Principal reduction will be $5,506.

How much is your tax liability?

First, deal with the Interest. All of it will be taxable, and the tax rate will by your individual tax rate, at the marginal level.

But the Principal that you receive will be taxed at the Capital Gains rate, at least part of it.

Some of the Down Payment will be included in first year Principal received.

Also includable in the first year Principal will be some of the Principal received as part of the monthly payments.

You must calculate your "ratio."

The Ratio is how much of the Sales Price is taxable as Capital Gains.

You bought for $30,000 and sold for $100,000, so your Capital Gains is $70,000.

This is 70% of the Sales Price, so as you receive Principal payments, 70% of each one represents Capital Gains (profit), while the other 30% is just the return or your original investment.

So, the total Principal received the first year is the $20,000 Down Payment and the $5,506 portion of monthly payments, for a total of $25,506.

And 70% of this (your "ratio") is $17,854 and that is your taxable Capital Gain.

Your tax rate will be either 0%, 15%, or 20%, and maybe a combination of two of those rates.

ANOTHER EXAMPLE

Same as the above scenario, except that what you bought instead of a tract of land was a rent house.

This is different because you did not claim any Depreciation with the land investment, but you did with the rental property.

And when you claim an annual Depreciation Allocation on rental property, you must deal with that fact when you sell the property, and you deal with it by paying a Depreciation Recapture tax on the amount claimed.

VOCABULARY OF TERMS

For the $30,000 rental property, you assigned $2,500 value to the land, and you depreciated the remaining $27,500 over 27.5 years, resulting in $1,000 a year in Depreciation.

So, over the ten years that you operated the rental property, you claimed $10,000 in Depreciation, and this reduced your Basis in the property from $30,000 to $20,000.

So, your Capital Gains is the difference between $20,000 and $100,000 and that is $80,000.

And the IRS requires you to pay a 25% Depreciation Recapture tax on the $10,000 before you pay the Capital Gains tax on the $70,000.

You received $25,506 in Principal in the first year, and 70% of it was profit, which is $17,854.

The first $10,000 of this is taxable as Depreciation Recapture at 25%, and the $7,854 is taxable at your individual Capital Gains Tax rate.

INTERIM FINANCING

Interim Financing is the loan that is obtained for a shorter period of time than a regular long-term loan.

It can be necessary for a variety of reasons.

The most common one is when a Builder is constructing a new residence or commercial building.

He needs to borrow money to pay for the materials and the labor.

When the project is completed, if he will continue to own the property, he will then apply for permanent long-term financing.

If he plans to sell the residence to a new owner, he will continue to pay monthly interest on the debt until the home is sold and the Buyer obtains permanent financing, at which time the Interim Financing is paid off.

If he plans to sell the commercial building to an investor or end-user, the same thing will happen.

Interim Financing can also be used for any relatively short period of time when funds are required to transition from one situation to another.

INTERNAL RATE OF RETURN (IRR)

Internal Rate of Return (IRR) is not "internal" and it is not a "rate of return."

It is also nearly impossible to calculate until after you have sold the investment.

IRR is defined as the Discount Rate (DR) for an investment applied to the Present Value (PV) of all future After-Tax Cash Flows (ATCF), and then compared to the cost of the Initial Capital Investment.

The ATCFs are yearly, but also include the sale of the investment property at some point in the future, usually at the end of ten years. The Net Sales Proceeds are added to the tenth year cash flow.

VOCABULARY OF TERMS

This process is almost complete guesswork, as you can see.

To make it more difficult, Your Discount Rate is defined as a combination of the Weighted Cost of Capital (WACC) and an assumed risk-free rate of return, which are normally set at 10% and 2%, but could really be anything, depending on who is doing the investing.

And if you are not already confused enough, you must also assume what the annual Cash Flow will be, and then discount that for each year back to the present to get the Present Value.

You must also predict what the investment will sell for ten years from now, and estimate what your transaction costs will be.

And, you must also predict what will happen to the tax laws for the next ten years, and factor that into the calculations.

The IRR looks impressive when you put it on a chart or graph, but the Internal Rate of Return Calculation is not worth very much.

And it is so complicated that there is not even a Calculation that you can use to test it.

And there are no Free Online Calculators that can handle this many unknowns.

So, what do you do instead?

The best thing for you to do is first perform a Discounted Cash Flow on the monthly income, and then calculate the Net Sales Proceeds from a sale in the future and discount that amount to the Present Value.

Then add the two numbers together and divide by the amount of your initial investment.

The main problem with the Internal Rate of Return Calculation is that it is a ratio, and that means that the investment must be cashed in so that you will have a number to compare with your initial investment.

So, it is not very useful for management purposes.

IRREVOCABLE TRUST

An Irrevocable Trust is a Trust which cannot be revoked by the person who set it up.

An Irrevocable Trust is really the only type of Trust that is a valid Trust under the law, since one of the legal requirements for a valid Trust is that the person setting up the Trust, called the Trustor or Grantor, must have no control or influence in the operation of the Trust once it is created. And, obviously, if the Trustor could revoke the Trust, that would constitute having control over the Trust.

So just by being a Trust, under the law, it is irrevocable.

It has become necessary to use the term "irrevocable" in describing a Trust because of the widespread use of another practice called a Living Trust, which is not really a Trust at all, for a number of reasons, but primarily because it can be revoked at any time for any reason or no reason, and without notice.

VOCABULARY OF TERMS

The so-called Living Trust is ambiguously referred to as a Revocable Trust, which is a pure oxymoron, since the thing cannot be a Trust in the first place if it is revocable.

See "Revocable Trust" for more information.

LATE FEES

Late Fees are not something that you can just impose because you own the property and because you call the shots.

Late Fees are like the amount of the rent, a matter to be agreed upon between the landlord and the tenant. And if you ever expect to have to enforce the collection with a legal proceeding, or avoid a charge of Usury lodged against you, the agreement must be in writing.

The Rental Agreement should spell out precisely how much the late fees will be. It can be a specific amount, or a percentage. But it must be one or the other.

If it is a specific amount, it should also state a time period, or time periods, associated with it, such as "$50 due and payable when the initial delinquency occurs, and an additional $50 for each month that the delinquency continues."

If the Late Fee is a percentage of the rent, it should be stated as such, and also state if it will continue for subsequent months that the delinquency continues.

The most important part of the late fee stipulation is exactly when the delinquency will occur, such as "midnight on the eighth day following the day that the rent is due."

Your Rental Agreement should state that the stated amount of rent is due and payable on a certain date "in full," and that payment of less than the full amount due will trigger the Late Fee.

The Agreement should also state that any monies received for rent will be applied first to delinquencies and late fees, and then to the current amount due. This will avoid an argument in Court about what the payment was being applied towards, when a payment was made.

Once the Late Fee is adequately spelled out in your Agreement, have the tenant sign it in front of a Notary Public. This avoids the situation where the tenant takes the Agreement away and brings it back with a forged signature, and this also avoids you having to prove the signature in Court.

You might also draw a line in the margin next to the paragraph about Late Fees, and have the tenant initial on the line. This will counter the argument later in Court when the Tenant says, "Yes, I read the Agreement, but I didn't see that."

With tenants, the time to deal with problems is before they occur.

VOCABULARY OF TERMS

LEASE-TO-OWN

"Lease-To-Own" is the popular term that is usually applied to the transaction more accurately known by the name of the document that evidences the deal, a "Lease With Purchase Option."

A Lease With Purchase Option is a combination of a Lease and an Option To Purchase.

You know what a Lease looks like, so we'll look at an Option To Purchase.

An Option To Purchase is a contractual right that you have which allows you to purchase a specific property at a specific date in the future for a specific price.

The date, instead of being a certain month, day, and year, might be something like 30 days after you have made payment number sixty, or something like that. But it is a date that can be determined with specificity.

The price, instead of being an exact dollar amount, might be a price that will be calculated using a certain formula, such as $100,000 less the total of 10% of each of the first 60 monthly lease payments.

An Option is usually something of value, and something for which you pay a price, provide a service, forego a right or opportunity, or provide a consideration.

In the case of a Lease With Option To Purchase, the consideration that you provide is to make five years of monthly payments on time.

If you fail to make all of the payments, on time, you will not be permitted to exercise the Option.

The Lease With Option To Purchase is one of those documents that are often litigated in Court, and the Court will often decide in favor of the Tenant, even when the terms have not been met exactly.

LIVING TRUST

See Revocable Trust.

LOAN MODIFICATION

A loan modification occurs when you and the Lender agree to change the terms of your loan.

Any of the terms can be changed, and a modified agreement can be signed.

The original loan is still in effect, the original collateral is still securing the loan, but something will be different.

The payment amount might be higher or lower.

The Stated Interest Rate might change.

The payments might be made every two weeks instead of monthly.

It is even possible for the Lender to allow the Borrower to pledge another asset to secure the loan, and have the lien released on the original property. But this would probably be handled with a procedure called "Substitution of Collateral," which is usually a separate agreement.

VOCABULARY OF TERMS

If the original loan is still "in house," meaning that the Lender (bank?) is still the owner of the loan, a modification is a possibility.

If the Lender has sold the loan on to another entity, or the loan has been packaged with a number of other loans, creating a product, to which multiple partial ownerships have been sold, then a loan modification is not possible.

MASS APPRAISAL

This is how the Tax Appraisal District and Taxing Authority usually assign a taxable value to a property.

They do not go out and look at each property.

They look at a printout with information about the property.

First, they collect enough data from a range of properties and do appraisals of those properties.

Then they identify each property with a set of characteristics and create a sample.

From there they apply that appraisal to every similar property, making slight adjustments for things like a two-car garage, or carport, or even an unpaved driveway.

Many appraisal offices do not have the budget or manpower to create their own database, so they use one that is created in Massachusetts.

MODIFIED ADJUSTED GROSS INCOME (MAGI)

Modified Adjusted Gross Income (MAGI) is an all-important number.

It determines your eligibility for all kinds of benefits and qualifications.

To determine your MAGI, first calculate your Adjusted Gross Income (AGI). You will find your AGI on line 8b of your Form 1040 for last year. Use that as a guide to estimate it for this year.

Now, add back:

1.) Deductions that you took for IRA contributions.

2.) Deductions that you took for taxable Social Security payments.

3.) Rental losses.

4.) Passive income or losses.

5.) Excluded foreign income.

6.) Half of Self-Employment (SE) taxes.

7.) Interest on EE Savings Bonds used to pay higher education expenses.

8.) Qualified tuition expenses.

9.) Exclusion for adoption expenses.

10.) Losses from publicly-traded partnerships.

11.) Deductions for student loan interest or tuition.

VOCABULARY OF TERMS

For most people, the MAGI will be the same number as their AGI, or very close.

PRESENT VALUE

Present Value is just what the term sounds like.

Present Value (PV) is the value of something today, usually a business asset, and usually with the value expressed in dollars.

The assets that we are interested in are real estate and money.

Your Duplex is worth $400,000.

Your CD is worth $100,000.

PV involves three elements: value, time, and a stated interest rate.

Value and time are usually determined by factors that are already in place.

That leaves the interest rate, and it is the key, and probably the most important of the three.

Think of this as the answer to the question: "How much money would you pay me in return for using $100,000 of my money for a year?"

If you would pay me $12,000 for that money, because you believe that you could use the money to make much more than that, then the annual time value of money, for you, is 12%.

You can use externally-determined interest factors if you want, such as the Federal Discount Rate, or the current maximum amount of interest available from the big banks on a $100,000 Certificate of Deposit.

That will tell you what others in the market are doing.

But you will get results that are more useful for you if you use a stated interest rate that is relevant to you and your business activities, or anticipated activities.

EXAMPLE

For Example, let's say that you are one of two owners of a Limited Liability Company (LLC) that owns an Apartment Building that is doing very well as an investment.

And someone offers to purchase your ownership interest in the LLC for $600,000 but cannot pay you the full amount up front. Instead, he offers you $100,000 now, $200,000 a year from now, and $300,000 two years from now, in three cash payments, with no interest accruing.

What is the PV of the $600,000 in total that you will receive over time?

Here is the Calculation for that.

And don't be afraid of it, you can do it, and you will be a better real estate investor after you become familiar with it.

VOCABULARY OF TERMS

$PV = A \div [(1 + R)$ MULTIPLIED BY ITSELF "N" NUMBER OF TIMES], WHERE

PV IS THE PRESENT VALUE,

A IS THE AMOUNT OF MONEY WE ARE DEALING WITH,

R IS THE STATED INTEREST RATE, AND

N IS THE NUMBER OF PERIODS WE ARE APPLYING THE CALCULATION.

It only looks difficult, so let's break it down.

First, the initial payment of $100,000 has a PV of $100,000 because you are receiving it now. We don't need the Calculation for that.

But the $200,000 that you will receive a year from now is a different matter.

You personally believe that the annual time value of money is 12%, so there is an amount of money that, if you had it now, and increased it by 12%, it would become $200,000 a year from now. You want to know what that amount of money is, because, for you, that is the value right now of the $200,000.

$PV = A \div (1 + R)$

$PV = 200{,}000 \div (1 + 0.12)$

$PV = 200{,}000 \div 1.12$

$PV = 178{,}571.43$

The Present Value of the $200,000 you will receive a year from now is $178,571.43.

See how that works? And it works every time.

What about the $300,000 you will receive in two years?

PV = A ÷ [(1 + R) x (1 + R)]

PV = 300,000 ÷ [(1 + 0.12) x (1 + 0.12)]

PV = 300,000 ÷ (1.12 x 1.12)

PV = 300,000 ÷ 1.2544

PV = 239,158.16

The Present Value of the $300,000 you will receive two years from now is $239,158.16.

That's quite a bit of difference!

The total Present Value of the $600,000 in three payment is 100,000 + 178,571.43 + 239,158.16 = $517,729.59.

As you can see, time and interest rate are the two most powerful factors at play in real estate investing.

All of your investment analysis should involve calculating the Present Value and its counterpart, the Future Value.

CALCULATOR

Now that you know what Present Value is, what it is used for, and how to use it, here is a Free Calculator you can use for quicker results.

VOCABULARY OF TERMS

https://www.calculatorsoup.com/calculators/financial/present-value-calculator-basic.php

1.) For "Number of Years" enter 1.0.

2.) For "Interest Rate" enter 12.0.

3.) For "Future Value" enter 200,000.

4.) Click "Calculate."

Your Present Value Calculation is $177,489.85.

As you can see, when we did the Calculation above with the same information, we got $178,571.43.

This is not a mistake.

We were compounding the interest rate annually, and the Calculator is compounding the interest rate monthly.

You must remember that the concept of Compound Interest works both ways.

Now, let's use the Calculator to determine the Present Value of the $300,000 that you will receive in two years.

1.) For "Number of Years" enter 2.0.

2.) For "Interest Rate" enter 12.0.

3.) For "Future Value" enter 300,000.

4.) Click "Calculate."

Your Present Value Calculation will be $236,269.84.

And again, you will notice that in our above Calculation we got $239,158.16 for Present Value.

And again, it is because the Calculator is using monthly compounding instead of yearly compounding.

If you ever want to double-check your answer when you do a Present Value Calculation, you can just reverse the process, and take the answer and treat it as the Present Value in a Future Value Calculation.

Here is the link for the Future Value Calculator.

https://www.calculatorsoup.com/calculators/financial/future-value-calculator-basic.php

These Calculations can be very helpful, and I refer you to one of my other books, "50 Real Estate Calculations," available in digital and print on Amazon.

OWNER FINANCING

See "Seller Financing."

PASS-THROUGH ENTITY

A Pass-Through Entity, referred to as a PTE, is a legal entity where the income earned by the entity is passed through to the owner or owners of the entity to be reported as income on their individual income tax returns.

A PTE might be an S Corp, a Partnership, or an LLC.

The S Corp will actually report the income on Form 1120S, and then provide each Shareholder with a Schedule K-1(1120S) and the K-1 will show the

VOCABULARY OF TERMS

individual their allocated share of the income, credits and allowances.

The Partnership will report the Partnership income on Form 1065, and then provide each Partner with a Schedule K-1(1065) showing the Partner's share of income, credits and allowances.

The LLC is a little different, depending on whether it has one owner or more than one, and because an LLC can actually elect to be treated as another type of entity for tax purposes.

If the LLC is a single-member LLC, called a SMLLC, does not file Form 8832, Entity Classification Election, the LLC will be given the default classification of "Disregarded Entity." This does not mean that the entity will be disregarded for tax purposes, it means that the IRS will disregard the fact that the individual formed the entity, and will treat the income of the LLC as though it were the income of the individual acting as a sole proprietor, and he will report the income on his personal tax return, Form C, or Form E, or Form F. Even though there is nothing passing through the LLC, the LLC that is a Disregarded Entity is still considered a PTE.

If the LLC is a SMLLC and files Form 8832 electing to be treated as an S Corp, it will act as an S Corp described above, and will be considered a PTE.

If the LLC is a SMLLC and files Form 8832 electing to treated for tax purposes as a C Corp, it will not be considered a PTE. The C Corp will file Form 1120 and will pay taxes on the income at the corporate level and retain the profit, which may or may not then be distributed to the single member as dividends.

If the LLC has more than one member, it is called a Multi-Member LLC (MMLLC), and if it does not file Form 8832, it is not defaulted to Disregarded Entity, but to Partnership status, because the members are look at by the IRS the same way they look at Partners. The LLC will be expected to file Form 1065 as described above. It will be considered a PTE.

If the MMLC does file Form 8832, it can elect to be treated for tax purposes as a Partnership, an S Corp, or a C Corp. If it becomes a Partnership or an S Corp, it will be considered a PTE, but not if it becomes a C Corp.

Being a PTE is important for a number of reasons, but primarily because it will probably qualify for the 20% Qualified Business Income (QBI) tax exemption on up to 20% of its income.

PERSONAL GUARANTY

A Personal Guaranty means that an individual is assuming personal liability for payment of a debt that is not his personal debt.

It often happens when a person has a legal entity such as an LLC, or a Partnership or Corporation, and that entity borrows money.

Usually the money is used for the purpose of buying real estate or another asset, or to make improvements on such an existing asset.

If the Lender feels that there is too much risk involved, the Lender will require the owner of the legal entity to personally guarantee the repayment of the loan.

VOCABULARY OF TERMS

This is not an unusual event.

But most people just sign the document that they are presented without question, thinking that their decision is to either do it or not do it.

But there are other ways to do the same thing.

What the Lender usually wants is a blanket guaranty, meaning that you, the Guarantor, are promising to repay the loan. This means that if a payment is missed, the Lender contacts you and you are expected to deal with the situation.

But you might be able to negotiate other options with the Lender.

You could become a Secondary Guaranty. This means that if the payment is late, the Lender deals with the entity. If the loan goes into default, the Lender pursues collection procedures against the entity leading up to posting the collateral for foreclosure. At this point you are required to take over and pay off the loan, in return for the Lender transferring to you the First Lien on the property that is securing the loan.

Or you could even become a Loss Guaranty. This means that the Lender deals with the entity all the way through foreclosure. If the Net Sales Proceeds from the Foreclosure Sale are not enough to pay off the loan, then you will make up the difference.

There is more than one kind of Guaranty, and it will benefit you to know the difference.

POINTS

"Points" are an additional fee charged by a Lender as part of the loan costs.

A Point means one percentage point, 1%.

So, if your Lender is offering you a Hard Money Loan of $50,000 for 6 months at 10% plus two Points, that does not mean that you will be paying 12% annual interest rate.

It means that in addition to paying 10% interest on the loan, you will pay another 2% up front, or $1,000.

You will notice that Points do not depend on any time period, like the interest rate.

Your 10% interest is an annual interest rate, so when you repay the $50,000 after six months, you would pay $2,500. That is 5% of the loan amount.

Points are a way for Lenders to charge a higher rate for shorter loans, and also to immediately recover some of the costs of handing the loan.

POWER OF ATTORNEY

A Power of Attorney is a document in which you give to another individual, not necessarily an Attorney, the right to perform an act that, otherwise, only you would be permitted to do.

For instance, you might authorize someone to sell real estate for you.

VOCABULARY OF TERMS

This document would be called a Special Power of Attorney For Real Estate Sale because it authorizes someone to do a special act on your behalf, but not anything else. It would detail specifically when, how, and where, and would contain details concerning amounts, etc.

A General Power of Attorney is a blanket authorization for another person to do anything and everything that you have the right to do on your own. The term used is that it is "like standing in the shoes" of the individual signing the Power of Attorney.

There are other types that are used in specific situations, such as a General Power of Attorney for Health Care, which authorizes decisions and acts as necessary regarding a specific area of your life, in this case, making medical decisions.

A Power of Attorney must be in writing. It does not have to be filed of public record, but often is, so that Certified Copies can be obtained to provide to anyone requiring proof of the authority to act.

A Power of Attorney can be revoked at any time by the person granting the power, and this is another reason to have it filed. The Revocation of Power of Attorney can then be filed to make sure that the general public knows that the power has been revoked.

A Power of Attorney can be written to take effect at some point in the future, either a specific date, or upon the occurrence of a specific event, such as the doctor-certified mental disability of the individual granting the power to another, usually a family member.

There is not a single "Power of Attorney."

Instead, it is a type of document that is used to accomplish a specific purpose.

So, if you just refer to "a Power of Attorney," you have not provided the information of "Which one?"

PRE-APPROVED

"Pre-Approved" is a term used by potential lenders when telling loan applicants the status of their loan application. It is usually just a ploy to keep the customer involved in the process.

"Pre-Approved" actually means that you have not been approved, and there is no reason to believe that you will be approved.

"Approved" means that you have been approved. Everything else means that you have not.

If the term means anything, it means that you have provided all of the documentation required.

The reason that you have not been turned down yet, and the reason that you have not been approved yet, is that the person or committee that will be making the decision on the loan application has not even seen your loan application package.

"Pre-Approved" is such a meaningless term that you will often receive a letter addressed to "Occupant" saying that you have been "Pre-Approved for 100% financing on a new" vehicle, along with no payments for three years, as well as a $5,000 Rebate.

VOCABULARY OF TERMS

PUBLIC NOTICE

Public Notice is a notice filed in the Public Records of the County where the individual resides or where the affected real estate is located.

Sometimes the filing of Public Notice is a legal requirement to complete the act itself.

Sometimes the filing of Public Notice is to give notice to the Public of a transaction, or a change of status, that is already a completed act, but must be filed in the public records in order to protect the interests of the parties involved.

For example, in some States, if you purchase property, you own that property if the Seller owned the property and signs a valid deed to you, and then delivers that deed to you. The final act of delivery of the deed completes the transfer of ownership.

But the Public does not know that you now own the property, and the Seller can go and sell the property to a second person, and the second person would be an "innocent purchaser for value" because there is no way that he could know that the Seller does not still own the property since his name is on the last deed recorded at the Courthouse on the property. That second person can then file his deed in the Public Records and he is the owner of the property.

So, sometimes the purpose of Public Notice is to protect the interest of a purchaser by giving notice to the Public that the property has changed hands.

In States such as the one referenced above, the legal concept is called "Race to the Courthouse."

QUITCLAIM DEED

See DEED.

REVOCABLE TRUST

A "Revocable Trust" is a very difficult concept to explain because there is so much misinformation about Trusts.

A Trust, by legal definition, is not revocable.

Therefore, there cannot be a thing called a "Revocable Trust."

But there is, because of the use of something called a "Living Trust."

The "living" was chosen by the people who promoted and marketed the scheme as a technique for Tax Planning and Estate Planning, with the primary objective of avoiding the requirement to Probate an Estate upon death.

But since "living" is not a legal term, and since it is necessary to accurately describe the planning device in legal terms, it had to be described as a Trust because there was an actual document, a Declaration of Trust.

But it also had to be further identified as "revocable" since that is its main distinguishing characteristic, and since that sets it apart from the standard legal definition of a Trust.

In practice, here is how a Revocable Trust works.

VOCABULARY OF TERMS

The Trustor sets up the Living Trust and names himself as the initial Trustee, and also names himself as the primary Beneficiary.

Both of these are not allowed in setting up a real Trust, so it does not meet the legal requirements to be a Trust, and it is not a Trust.

The language of the Declaration of Trust says that the Trust can be revoked at any time, which is also prohibited with a real Trust.

But, and this is the key to the whole scheme, the language also says something to the effect of "upon my death this Revocable Trust shall become Irrevocable, and I name Helen Jones as Successor Trustee, and I name the children of Helen Jones as the Successor Beneficiaries."

At this point, the illegal Revocable Trust immediately becomes a legal Irrevocable Trust.

And if the Trustor put all of his assets into the Trust, then he has nothing that needs to pass through Probate, and the time and expense of such a proceeding is avoided.

When done properly, it is an effective Tax Planning and Estate Planning tool.

But there are a lot of potential problems.

The first problem involves trying to deed real estate to the Revocable Trust.

Since it is not a valid legal Trust, it does not exist as a legal entity and therefore cannot own real estate.

And even if it could, real estate that is going into a real, legal, Trust is not deeded to the Trust, it is deeded to the Trustee.

And since the person who set up the Living Trust named himself as Trustee, he would be deeding the property to himself as Trustee of a Revocable Trust that has no legal existence.

There are many other legal problems as well, with brokerage accounts and retirement accounts, but people just seem to ignore them and pretend that everything is fine.

If you decide to use a Living Trust in spite of everything, PLEASE, get one from an Attorney who specializes in Estate Planning, instead of from a Salesman.

RIGHT OF SURVIVORSHIP

A Right of Survivorship is a right that is granted by one person to another to automatically become the owner of the first person's interest upon the death of the first person, usually referring to the ownership rights that the two parties are holding together in an asset, and which is usually real estate.

In many situations, at the time that you take title to real estate, you elect the manner in which you wish to hold title, and then you use a document that will vest that type of ownership in you.

When you take title to real estate along with another person, one of the types of ownership that the two of

VOCABULARY OF TERMS

you can choose is called "Joint Tenancy With Right of Survivorship."

Now, don't be confused by the "tenancy" word. It does not have anything to do with residing on the property. "Joint Tenancy" just means owning the property together.

If you take title as Joint Tenancy With Right of Survivorship, that means that when one of you dies, the other becomes the owner of 100% interest in the property.

SELLER FINANCING

Seller Financing happens when the Owner of real estate sells the property to the Buyer, and instead of receiving the Sales Price in cash, the Owner agrees to take a Down Payment and then receive monthly payments representing the accrued interest, and the monthly reduction of principal, until the total Principal Amount is paid.

In effect, the Owner is becoming the Bank, or Lender, and is providing the financing on the sale of the property for the Buyer.

That's why it is also called "Owner Financing."

Seller Financing is often used by Sellers to gain an advantage in the market because many Buyers will prefer to deal with a property where they do not have to go to the Bank and jump through hoops, and the Seller will have more people immediately inquiring about the property.

Seller Financing can also create a disadvantage because the Seller will have to deal with potential Buyers who are not qualified to receive the financing, and have been turned down by the Bank, and will usually end up just wasting the Seller's time.

But for most Buyers and for most Sellers, Seller Financing is a great advantage for both.

STEPPED-UP BASIS

The concept of Stepped-up Basis is one of the five most important things for you to understand if you expect to have long-term success in real estate investing.

People shy away from learning about it because they think it is too difficult.

It is not, and I think the following will explain it to you.

FOR INDIVIDUAL TAXPAYERS

A step-up in Basis happens when the owner of the property dies, and the property is inherited either through the probate of a Will or the administration of an intestate estate, or the property goes into a Trust.

Internal Revenue Code Section 1014, entitled "Basis Of Property Acquired From A Decedent," provides that the Basis of a Decedent's property will be changed (usually increased) to its Fair Market Value (FMV) as of the Date of Death (DOD).

That means that there is a step-up in Basis when a person dies and leaves property to an heir.

VOCABULARY OF TERMS

The step-up in Basis will usually mean that the person inheriting the property can sell it without having to pay any Capital Gains Tax because the amount that he sells it for will usually be the FMV, and his Basis in the property is also the FMV.

That's what the step-up in Basis does, raise the Basis to the FMV.

The real value of the Stepped-up Basis comes from using Section 1031 Exchanges for your entire lifetime to defer the Capital Gains taxes, and then passing your property to your heirs, and wiping out all of the deferred Capital Gains.

You might have started with an investment in a property with a Basis of $50,000 and, through a series of Section 1031 Exchanges and financing, now have property worth $1,000,000 but with a Basis of less than $100,000.

With a Capital Gains rate of 20%, the step-up in Basis will avoid a tax bill of about $180,000.

After deferring taxes on Capital Gains and Depreciation Recapture for your entire life, the "pot of gold at the end of the rainbow" is to pass the property to your heirs, and eliminate all of your tax liability.

Stepped-up Basis turns the "tax-deferred" taxes from all of your past sales into "tax-free" for your heirs.

However, there is a big difference between holding title to the property in your own name, and owning the property through a business entity.

You might still be entitled to claim a Stepped-up Basis if you hold the property through a business entity, but it will depend on the business entity in which you are holding the property.

FOR BUSINESS ENTITIES

If you are not holding real property in your own name, then Partnerships and LLCs are the best business entities to use.

The LLC can elect for tax purposes to be treated as either a disregarded entity, a partnership, a C Corp, or an S Corp.

You should not elect to be treated as a C Corp.

By taking an Internal Revenue Code Section 754 election upon the death of a shareholder, the Partnership or LLC gets a step-up in Basis for the property in the hands of the Deceased.

For Example, let's assume that you and your brother set up a Corporation and each of you put in $50,000, and each of you own 50% of the stock. The corporation buys a warehouse for $100,000.

Ten years later, you die and leave everything to your son, and the warehouse is worth $1,000,000.

Your son will receive a Stepped-up Basis in the value of the corporate stock.

But the corporation will not receive a Stepped-up Basis in the value of the warehouse. The warehouse is owned by the corporation, and the corporation did not die. If the warehouse is sold, the corporation will

VOCABULARY OF TERMS

owe taxes on $900,000 of Capital Gains. (Including an unknown amount for Depreciation Recapture Tax). In effect, your son will pay half of the taxes because it will come out of his half of the corporation's funds.

Now, let's assume that you and your brother set up an LLC instead of a corporation, and that everything else is the same. The LLC will be treated for tax purposes as a Partnership because there is more than one owner.

When you die, the LLC makes a Section 754 election, and the son's share of the LLC assets receives a Stepped-up Basis to $500,000.

If the LLC sells the warehouse, the son will have no Capital Gains taxes to pay. If the LLC does not sell the warehouse, the son has a Basis of $500,000 inside the LLC which he can depreciate.

FOR HUSBANDS AND WIVES

If a Husband and Wife own the real estate together, and one of them dies, the survivor will receive a Stepped-up Basis in the share owned by the deceased spouse, but may not in their own share.

It depends on where they live and how they hold title.

In States that do not have the Community Property law, if the real estate is held in Joint Tenancy, and one spouse dies, the surviving spouse will received a Stepped-up Basis in the share of the property inherited from the deceased spouse, but not in the share already owned. This share retains its Cost Basis.

In Community Property states, the opposite is true.

If the surviving spouse inherits the property, all of the property receives a Stepped-up Basis.

Taking an Example of a $300,000 property, if the Community Property surviving spouse sold it shortly after the death of her spouse for $500,000, there would be no Capital Gains tax because the Sales Price would be the same as the Stepped-up Basis.

But if the Joint Tenancy surviving spouse did the same, her Basis in the property would be $150,000, half of the Cost Basis of $300,000, plus $250,000, the Stepped-up Basis of the share that she inherited from the deceased spouse, for a total Basis of $400,000.

The Joint Tenancy surviving spouse would have a $100,000 Capital Gains tax liability.

Community Property states are:

- Arizona,
- California,
- Idaho,
- Louisiana,
- Nevada,
- New Mexico,
- Texas,
- Washington, and
- Wisconsin.

Alaska allows spouses to opt-in to a Community Property arrangement.

VOCABULARY OF TERMS

SUBORDINATE FINANCING

Subordinate Financing is the debt that is placed on the property after the Primary Financing is completed, usually being secured by a First Lien on the property.

The Subordinate Financing will usually involve the construction of improvements, or involve undertaking major repairs or rehabilitation, and the debt will be secured by a Second Lien on the property.

A Lender would be willing to extend Subordinate Financing because if the project is large enough, the Owner already has enough equity in the property to mitigate the risk.

The investor might buy an apartment complex for $1M, and get a loan for $800,000.

That means that he already has $200,000 in equity, usually the amount of his Down Payment.

A Lender would be willing to loan him another $200,000 to do the necessary repairs and improvements if that would probably bring the value of the property up to about $1.5M, because he knows that if he does not get paid and has to foreclose on the property, he will be getting an asset worth $1.5M.

Of course, he will have to take it with the $800,000 debt from the Primary Financing, but he has still acquired $700,000 equity for an investment of $200,000 plus the lost interest payments and the legal cost.

Some Lenders even specialize in doing Subordinate Financing.

SUBSTITUTION OF COLLATERAL

Collateral is what you pledge as security when you obtain a loan from a bank or from a private lender.

In the case of real estate, it is usually when you borrowed money to purchase the property, or you went from Interim Construction Financing while you were building a structure, into Permanent Financing.

The loan procedure creates a lien on the real estate, and the lien secures the payment of the loan.

It is less common today to have a situation where the collateral securing a loan is changed, except in some commercial situations.

But the process is still done.

All of the terms of the loan will remain the same, but at some point the Borrower might want to substitute another piece of property for the property securing the loan.

If the Lender is a Private Lender, or if the Lender is a Bank where the loan has been kept "in-house" and the Bank has the flexibility to do it, a Substitution of Collateral Agreement can accomplish just that, with everything else remaining the same.

It involves much less time than obtaining a new loan on the new property and using the proceeds to pay off the loan on the existing property.

VOCABULARY OF TERMS

TITLE INSURANCE

"Title Insurance" is the insurance coverage that you receive when you purchase a piece of real estate, and it covers the condition of the title to the property.

The complete name is "Owner's Policy of Title Insurance" and is referred to as an Owner's Policy.

Title Insurance is different from other kinds of insurance like automobile insurance, which insures you against future events.

Title Insurance insures you against past events.

The policy says that if you suffer a loss due to a past defect in the title of the property, you will be reimbursed for your loss.

A Title Insurance Policy does not guarantee that title to the property is free and clear, which is a popular misconception.

All property has some questions regarding title. The Title Insurance Company determines if the risk associated with those questions is worth taking, and if it is, the policy is issued. If it is not, the policy will exclude certain items and the consumer and Lender decides whether to accept these exclusions.

A Title Insurance Policy does not travel with the property when it is sold.

The new Owner will receive a new Title Insurance Policy.

Associated with the Owner's Policy of Title Insurance is another policy called a Lender's Policy of Title Insurance. It insures the Lender against any loss caused by a defect in the title. That's why the Lender is involved in the decision-making process.

TITLE OPINION

A Title Opinion is the opinion of someone regarding the condition of title to a piece of real estate.

It is usually the opinion of someone with some expertise regarding real estate law, such as an Attorney.

It is not a guarantee or a warranty of title. It is just an opinion.

Title Insurance Companies do not do a Title Opinion, they issue a Title Insurance Policy which insures against loss caused by a defect in title. The policy is not an opinion as to the condition of title. The policy is a willingness to assume any risk associated with any potential defect in the title which might result in a problem.

Other terms used in this regard are "Certificate of Title Opinion" and "Certificate of Title," but neither of them is a guarantee of clear, or even marketable, title.

If you do not have a Policy of Title Insurance, all you have is an opinion, even if it is being called a "certificate."

VOCABULARY OF TERMS

VALUE

Value is a matter of opinion, of course, and this is the core of why real estate changes hands, and the basis of how profits are made.

Real estate will usually have a value for you that is different from the value that it has for someone else.

And there are Calculations for you to determine those values.

WHAT THE PROPERTY IS WORTH TO YOU

You can calculate value based on what the property is worth to you, or what the property is worth to anyone like you who seeks a specific return on investment, or seeks a specific Cap Rate.

You do this by calculating the Economic Value of the property.

V = NOI ÷ CR, where

V is the Economic Value,

NOI is the Net Operating Income, and

CR is the Capitalization Rate

If you are looking at a property that produces $3,000 per month of net income from operations, then your NOI will be $36,000.

If you are expecting to earn a 10% rate of return on your investment, then your CR will be 10% (0.10).

Therefore:

V = NOI ÷ CR

V = 36,000 ÷ 0.10

V = 360,000.

This property will have an Economic Value to you of $360,000.

WHAT YOUR PROPERTY IS WORTH TO SOMEONE ELSE

You can also use the Value calculation to determine what your property will be worth to someone else. Just find out what that person's expected Cap Rate is and plug it into the calculation.

Chances are, there is a similar target Cap Rate that is being used by the general community of real estate investors for a particular type of property.

If you know this number, and you have a property for sale, you will be able to determine what someone would be willing to pay for it.

Let's say you have a multi-family property, a 10-unit apartment building, and your NOI based on the last twelve months of operation is $45,000.

If multi-family investors in your area are currently willing to accept a 6% Cap Rate, then your calculation is:

V = NOI ÷ CR

V = 45,000 ÷ 0.06

VOCABULARY OF TERMS

V = 750,000

You would be safe to market your property for $750,000 and expect to be negotiating with serious buyers.

HOW TO DETERMINE THE CAP RATE

In the above Example, you might want to get an advantage in the market by promoting your property as the one that is offering a higher Cap Rate than the other properties available.

Let's say that you are willing to take $710,000 for the property, and wonder if that will raise the Cap Rate enough to get buyers' attention.

This is the Calculation to determine the Cap Rate:

CR = NOI ÷ V, WHERE

CR IS THE CAP RATE,

NOI IS THE NET OPERATING INCOME, AND

V IS THE ECONOMIC VALUE OF THE PROPERTY

CR = NOI ÷ V

CR = 45,000 ÷ 710,000

CR = 0.634

Lowering your asking price to $710,000 would allow you to market the property as having a Cap Rate of 6.34%.

LOAN TO VALUE RATIO

Another way in which the term "Value" is used is when a Lender is determining how much of a Down Payment will be required if you want to finance the purchase of an investment property.

That Calculation for Loan-to-Value Ratio is

$LVR = LA \div V$, WHERE

LVR IS THE LOAN-TO-VALUE RATIO,

LA IS THE LOAN AMOUNT, AND

V IS THE LESSER OF THE SELLING PRICE OR THE APPRAISED VALUE.

Let's say you find a Fourplex with an asking price of $400,000 and both the tax records and the NOI support the price, but it needs work and you sign a contract for $360,000.

Your Lender has promised a 70% loan.

How much will you be able to borrow?

$LVR = LA \div V$

$.70 = LA \div 360,000$

$.70 \times 360,000 = LA$

$252,000 = LA$

$LA = 252,000$

VOCABULARY OF TERMS

Your Loan Amount will be $252,000 based on a Loan-to-Value Ratio of 70%, when the Value is identified as the lesser of the Fair Market Value or the Selling Price.

So, Value is used in a number of different ways, and all are correct within the context of their use.

There are even two different types of Appraised Value, and both are correct.

The Taxing Authority will do what they call a Tax Appraisal, which is placing a Value on your property so that the Property Tax Rate can be applied and the amount of your Property Taxes determined.

Tax Appraisals were once wildly inaccurate because they were being done by unqualified, virtually-untrained employees, because it was a low-paying government job.

Today, the process is done by a very good computer program using a database of historic data, and the appraisals are much more accurate.

The other type of Appraised Value is an Appraisal, hopefully done by a licensed Appraiser, and including a multi-page report with comparable sales ("comps") and pictures of all properties, and an explanation of how the Appraised Value was determined.

These also used to be wildly inaccurate, but now that some of those people have gone to jail for being part of a process of defrauding Lenders, it is almost impossible to get anything but a totally accurate Appraisal.

CALCULATOR

Now that you understand the various ways to look at Value, let's use a Free Calculator to determine Value based on your Capitalization Rate.

https://www.ajdesigner.com/php_capitalization_rate/capitalization_rate_v.php

1.) For "net operating income (NOI)" enter 36000 (no comma).

2.) For "capitalization rate (CR)" enter 10.

3.) Click "Calculate."

Your Value is Calculated to be $360,000.

This is the same number that we got when doing it by hand.

You can substitute various factors here and see exactly what investment numbers you need to meet your objectives.

VOID

Void means that something happened, but is of no effect. It is as though it never happened, and that whatever is being attempted will not result.

For instance, if you sign an Affidavit and file it in the Real Property Records declaring that a certain tract of land is hereby zoned R-3, Multi-family Residential, that action would be void because you don't have the authority to do that.

VOCABULARY OF TERMS

But there is another term to be aware of, and it is called "voidable."

A voidable act is an action that is not void on its face, but if it is challenged and found not to have met the legal requirements for taking it, the Courts will void the action.

An example would be a forged signature on a document, or filing a counterfeit document.

In some cases, a voidable act can be voided just by the filing of other documents in contravention of it.

An example would be the filing of a Lien Affidavit which is allegedly based on the provisions of a specific ordinance, and then have a City Manager file an Affidavit stating that such actions are not authorized under that specific ordinance.

The area of law concerning voidable acts is too complicated to explain briefly, just be aware that simply because someone has filed something does not mean that it is a legitimate and final act.

And there is a difference between acts that are "void," and acts that are "voidable."

WRAPAROUND FINANCING

Wraparound Financing is when you sell real estate on which you already have a loan, without paying off that loan, and in selling the real estate, you finance the sale to the new Buyer.

The new Buyer pays you monthly payments and you continue to make the monthly payments on your existing loan.

You "wrap" the new financing "around" the existing financing.

This can only happen if your existing Mortgage or Deed of Trust does not have a "due on sale" clause, or it has one and you ignore it and the Lender has not found out about it yet.

Either way, your new transaction must be with the full knowledge and agreement of the new Buyer concerning the existing financing staying in place.

The Buyer will agree to accept the property "subject to" the existing debt, and will give you a Second Lien to secure his payment to you of his obligation, while the original Lender retains the First Lien which is securing the original financing.

In theory, when the new Buyer pays off his obligation to you, you will pay off your obligation to the original Lender, obtain a Release of Lien of the First Lien, provide the new Buyer with a Release of Lien of the Second Lien, and the new Buyer will own the property free and clear.

The new Buyer might also obtain other financing at some point and cause this same process to take place.

VOCABULARY OF TERMS

A FINAL WORD

I hope you have found the words, terms, concepts, and ideas in this book beneficial.

I have five other books about various aspects of Real Estate Investing and I invite you to go to:

amazon.com/Michael-Lantrip/e/B01N2ZRGUY

and take a look at them.

Click on the "Look Inside" feature and check out the Table of Contents and read the Introduction and a couple of Chapters.

I appreciate your time, and I wish you every success.

MICHAEL LANTRIP

VOCABULARY OF TERMS

MICHAEL LANTRIP

Made in the USA
Coppell, TX
23 January 2021